MW01708983

Letters From Sugar

Letters From Sugar

Joyce Ernyes

Illustrated by Lesley Bergen

SIT JACK PUBLISHING

This edition published in Canada in 2016 by Sit Jack Publishing
sitjackpublishing.ca

This is a work of fiction. Any references to real people, real places, real pets, or events are used fictitiously. Other names, characters, places and events are creations of the author's imagination and any resemblance to actual events, places or persons living or dead is entirely coincidental.

Library and Archives Canada Cataloguing in Publication

Ernyes, Joyce, author
Letters from Sugar / Joyce Ernyes; illustrated by Lesley Bergen.

ISBN 978-0-9939231-0-4 (paperback)

I. Title.

Sit Jack Publishing
7 Guardhouse Dr.
Bolton, ON
Canada L7E 5W7
sitjackpublishing.ca

Cover and text design: Marijke Friesen
Cover and interior illustrations: Lesley Bergen

Printed and Bound in Canada

FSC www.fsc.org MIX Paper from responsible sources FSC® C016245

To Guszti

Your gentle spirit, warm smile and kindness to animals will always be remembered.

"There are two means of refuge from
the misery of life: music and cats."
Albert Schweitzer

Contents

A New Home For Sugar 1
Mother's Day 11
The Royal Wedding 17
Father's Day 23
Bad Hair Day 29
Sugar Visits The Big City 35
Halloween 43
Grey Cup 49
'O Sole Mio 57
Home Alone 63
Adventures At The Bulrush Boarding Kennel 69
A Dog Named Chesapeake 81
Cuda Writes To Sugar 91
Sugar Writes To Cuda 101
The Tooth 109
Sugar's Great Escape Caper . . . Well, maybe not quite! 117
Dijon 129
Lester 137
The Tobacco Shack Cats 145
Dear Tabby 155
Spice 165

A New Home For Sugar

Dear Mom & Dad,

Thus far, time, by human measurement eludes me. I can only relate to its passage by the light of day and the darkness of night. That being said, I believe I have been at my new home for approximately thirty daylights. Hopefully at some point in the future I will understand the concept of weeks, months, years and a period of time referred to as a fortnight.

With little to do until the weather is more to my liking and I can venture outdoors, I have decided to try my paw at writing you a letter using the computer. I have had to enlist the help of my adoptive family members, however, since it has been brought to my attention that there is no spell-check or translation for feline vocabulary . . . yet!

Where to begin? Perhaps I should start by telling you about the journey from your house to my new home — it was quite eventful!

Despite your assurances that I would be well cared for by my new family, I was nevertheless frightened and apprehensive when departure time came. For the first part of the voyage I cowered in the far corner of my carry cage, protesting vehemently by way of long mournful meowels, punctuated with an occasional hiss for good measure.

Wesley and Jenna tried to calm me by talking to me in soothing, reassuring tones but I continued to object! They were no doubt having second thoughts about their decision to adopt me.

It was eventually decided that Jenna would remove me from my confinement and hold me in her arms. I presume they reasoned that if I felt more secure in my surroundings the meoweling might cease and Wesley could better concentrate on the task of driving on the busy highway. He stopped on the side of the road to facilitate this manoeuvre.

I did, in fact, feel more comfortable with this arrangement and my anxiety began to subside. We continued on but not for long. As we were approaching a winding curve in the road, the flow of traffic got progressively slower until we finally came to a complete stop. It was obvious that a problem existed on the road ahead.

As drivers exited their cars and began milling about, Wesley learned that a transport truck was on fire and it would be quite some time before the debris would be cleared from the roadway. Apparently no one was injured, but it was a frightening scene to witness as flames and smoke billowed upwards as high as the tree tops. Lights of various colours were flashing and twirling in the distance while more vehicles arrived at great speeds emitting loud piercing sounds.

With nothing to do but sit and wait, time passed slowly. When Jenna's arms began to tire from holding me and I was obviously drifting towards sleep, she returned me to my carry cage ... ever so gently. The rationale being that "a sleeping cat is a quiet cat."

I did sleep peacefully for quite a while but I awoke as our vehicle began to move slowly forward. Thankfully we were on our way. The journey, which should have taken two hours in Wesley's estimation, had now stretched to three and we were still far from home.

My tummy rumbled . . . a hunger pang no doubt! Then, a horrifying thought occurred to me. "What if the need arises and I am required to utilize my litter box before arriving at our destination?" I was aware that a small disposable facility had been placed in the back half of my oversized carry cage, but to actually have to use it within the confines of the family car was unthinkable. To add to my distress a heavy rain had begun falling and all windows had been closed tightly.

I won't elaborate on the situation that ensued, but suffice to say . . . Murphy's Law prevails in the animal kingdom as well!

Arriving at my new home, I was greeted with enthusiasm by Jason. (Wesley and Jenna were kind enough not to mention my en route behaviour.) I sensed that Jason liked cats and we bonded immediately.

I am happy to report that I adjusted very quickly to my new surroundings. The house is quite spacious with stairs connecting three levels of living area. This design affords some degree of physical exercise in my otherwise sedentary life. There are also many soft chairs and sofas throughout the house, which I have repeatedly tested for comfort and flexibility of purpose. Surfaces within close proximity of my food bowl take precedence.

An abundance of windows with wide sills provide vantage points from which I can enjoy a panoramic view of gardens on all sides of the house. Although I have yet to see a sign of grass sprouting or leaves budding on shrubs and trees, the increased activity among the rodent population has not gone unnoticed.

With the slight hint of spring in the air, the outside temperature is beginning to rise, thus triggering the shedding of my winter fur. My adoptive family members, not being accustomed to sharing their home with a feline, have been somewhat negligent in scrutinizing seating areas for cat hair before sitting down. This oversight occurred recently with potentially disastrous repercussions. Thus was the scenario: Early one Saturday morning, I was awakened by a flurry of activity in the vicinity of Jason's room. Being true to my species, curiosity got the better of me and I ventured closer to his bedroom door in order to determine what had provoked such an early rise on a "sleep in" day. Moments later Jason emerged dressed in a black tuxedo. A final check in the hallway mirror reflected a look of perfection. I overheard the words, "friend's wedding" and "best man" as he spoke into his cell phone.

A glance at his watch confirmed that it wasn't quite departure time, so he settled himself on the living room sofa…in the spot I had just vacated. To acknowledge his presence, I rubbed affectionately against his lower legs and in turn I was rewarded with a hug and a chin scratch.

Shortly thereafter, the doorbell rang signalling the arrival of his transportation. As he stood to leave, I stared in disbelief. This tall, handsome, (previously) well-groomed young man, who exuded the confidence of a GQ model, was covered in a film of pale grey cat hair from head to toe. With mere seconds remaining before he exited the door, I lunged towards him, rubbing aggressively against his pant legs in the hope that a departing pat on my head would alert him to his predicament. Unfortunately, my antics served only to deposit more hair on his lower extremities.

Needless to say, when Jason arrived at his destination, just prior to the ceremony, the condition of his formal attire was a serious cause for concern. Murphy being in attendance (once again) precluded anyone from being in possession of a clothes brush!

I suspect that one of my lives may have been saved, however, by the discovery of a roll of masking tape which was left behind by the decorating committee. Relief washed over me as Jason described the next sequence of events upon his return home.

Apparently with only minutes to spare until the sound of "Here Comes the Bride" would fill the air, lengths of masking tape were ripped from the roll and a blur of hands, belonging to all seven bridesmaids, the mother of the groom, and the flower girl, proceeded to dab the sticky side of the tape to every inch of the tuxedo while Jason sat coatless and pantless behind an arbour of purple and white chrysanthemums.

Since then I have been receiving regular brushings and I am *encouraged* to take naps in one of my two sleeping baskets. I am, nevertheless, keeping a low profile until the above incident is no longer a topic of conversation around the dinner table.

Thank you for finding a patient and understanding family to adopt me.

Love & Puurrrs,
Sugar

Mother's Day

ACME DECOY

Dear Mom,

It was nice of you and Dad to call, inquiring as to my well-being. I am actually in quite good health, as was confirmed recently by my new veterinarian. Doctor Emerson seemed genuinely caring and made inquiries about my medical history. His assistant Sarah commented on how well behaved I was throughout my examination. I do wish, however, that there could be found a more dignified way of taking a cat's temperature.

Since the arrival of spring and thus warmer weather, I have been spending leisurely afternoons outdoors while Jenna attends to the many gardens on the property. Beyond the landscaped area there is a forest that separates our home from others in the vicinity and this densely treed strip of land is also home to a variety of wildlife species. It is, therefore, a requirement that I am always accompanied when I am outdoors and I must stay within the boundaries of our property.

Jenna has befriended a chipmunk who arrives daily to watch her trim, weed, plant and rake. I suspect his visits have more to do with the pocket full of peanuts that she carries around and doles out to him throughout the day. I have offered to "guard" the peanuts but Jenna says I must stay at least five metres away from him at all times. Likewise, birds' nests are off limits. She sure can be a pain in the butt . . . even more so than the thermometer.

Wesley has been bedridden for a few days with a "bad cold" (his words). Jenna says to use the word *bad* is redundant as there is no other kind of cold. She remarked that this quasi rationale also applies to the size of snakes that she encounters from time to time. There is only one size . . . LARGE!

A heron, or perhaps herons, have once again been patrolling the two ponds on our property. It is difficult to determine how many are partaking of the smorgasbord of fish and frogs since only one at a time has been observed.

A variety of measures were put in place by Wesley and Jenna in the hope of discouraging the birds' daily dining routine, but to no avail. With but a handful of koi remaining in each pond, a more calculated approach had to be taken and two decoy herons were purchased, one being placed at each waters' edge. Seemingly these large birds are territorial and will be discouraged from entering another heron's feeding area. An exception to that philosophy was quickly realized one morning during mating season. I won't elaborate.

Happy Mother's Day!

Puurrrs,
Sugar

The Royal Wedding

OOK OF CATS &
GARDENING

Dear Mom & Dad,

I am now feeling slightly more comfortable on the computer and look forward to a time when I will no longer require any human assistance.

I am still somewhat baffled by the technical devices humans have come to rely upon, the computer being one and the television another. Although in this household the "TV" as I've heard it called, is seldom turned on, I do marvel at the concept of someone pressing a few buttons and instantly accessing a variety of moving pictures with sound effects. Compounding my confusion, I was recently introduced to a "recording."

One afternoon the family gathered in the living room and a small disk-like object was inserted into an opening beneath the television; more button pushing occurred and everyone sat back with looks of great expectations as the images on the TV screen came to life. Amazing! We were now observing an event that had already occurred sometime in the past. An added benefit to this recording technology is that the action can be stopped at any time and restarted without missing dialogue. No more waiting for a commercial in order to be fed.

Seemingly, my family members were familiar with the subject matter that had been recorded, so initially there was little conversation to enlighten me as to what we were observing. Recalling recent news bulletins, I assumed that another far-away government was about to be overthrown. Why else would thousands of people be gathered in the streets screaming and waving their arms in the air?

Fortunately, Jenna's young nephew, Simon, was visiting and the answers to his many questions served to inform me as well.

The event we were watching was in fact a Royal Wedding. This memorable ceremony, explained

Jenna, would unite two people who will likely, one day, become the King and Queen of England.

Simon made an interesting observation. The bride and groom were travelling in a horse-drawn buggy with very large wooden wheels and no roof. My heart was saddened at the thought that perhaps this young couple could not afford a motorized vehicle.

There was also some dialogue regarding the men in red attire that were referred to as Palace Guards. Simon was in awe of the very large black objects these men were balancing on their heads. I quickly recognized the fact that these elaborate headdresses were made of fur — which I suspect had once belonged to a black bear. I do hope that cat-hair accessories never become de rigueur for special occasions.

It was obvious, even to me, that a great deal of planning would be required to orchestrate such a spectacular event — preparing the guest list, choosing the menus, organizing transportation and accommodation, selecting appropriate music, etc. My guess is, however, that the most daunting task facing the organizers would have been the seating arrangement in Westminster Abbey. They would have had to ensure (discreetly) that guests wearing monstrous hats would not be seated within a metre of each other. An embarrassing entanglement of haute couture could have otherwise ensued. Likewise vertically challenged individuals would have had to be positioned (very discreetly) next to those wearing head gear sprouting long feathers of fowl and other antenna-like projections. An oversight of this magnitude could result in a serious eye injury providing grounds for litigation.

Security had to have been a major concern as well, at such a high-profile event. My feline intuition told me that some of those hats were in fact concealing satellite receivers worn by undercover agents, and Camilla's enormous disk-shaped chapeau was no doubt home base.

This wedding ceremony was quite lengthy and extended well beyond my nap time but the periodic ear and chin rubs from Simon more than compensated for my sleep deprivation.

I hope you are both well.

Puurrrs,
Sugar

Father's Day

Dear Dad,

I overheard Wesley and Jenna discussing your unfortunate fall, which resulted in a rather serious fracture to your right foot. I hope the pain has eased and you are feeling better.

I was reminded recently that I have now been with my adoptive family for several months. I haven't yet determined how many daylights that is, but they seem to be flying by. Wesley confided to me that time appears to pass more quickly as we grow older.

According to Dr. Emerson I am approaching middle age, but he qualified that I am nevertheless in remarkably good shape. He noted that I have excellent posture, good flexibility in my hind legs, and my tail wagging ability is second to none! My ego has been further sustained by Wesley's observation that my exceptional hearing allows me to detect the rustle of a treat bag opening from three floors down — even when I'm asleep.

My outdoor activities were severely curtailed recently due to a rather long period of unfavourable weather in our area. Everyone is thankful that the rain has finally subsided . . . especially me! Not long ago, someone remarked to Wesley that if the rain continued much longer, Noah would have to build another Ark. I had a few sleepless nights contemplating that statement . . . my fear being that I would be left behind given that my reproductive capability was taken from me at a young age.

The excessive rain was also a hindrance to Jenna and her garden maintenance schedule. Not only was she unable to work in the inclement weather, but the weeds flourished in the warm moist conditions. Plant-eating insects returned as well, with insatiable appetites, in the absence of her homemade bug repellent, which was washed away with the first deluge of rain.

Wesley, always positive in his outlook when adversity presents itself, suggested contacting the editors of a gardening magazine with a proposal of sorts. Being that our gardens no doubt harbour every type of insect, caterpillar, plant-eating bug and weed that exist in the province, he reasoned that any horticultural publication (for a nominal fee) would be grateful for the opportunity to photograph all species in one convenient location. Jenna is seriously considering the suggestion.

Jason just got up and is looking for me so I had better put on my "I'm hungry" look. I always lick my bowl clean so he doesn't suspect that I have already been fed. (Tee-hee!)

I hope you will have a very enjoyable Father's Day despite your restricted mobility.

Puurrrs,
Sugar

Bad Hair Day

ODOUR REM
SKunk
Be
Gon

Dear Mom & Dad,

We are presently experiencing the extreme heat and humidity of summer. Even my outdoor shade spots no longer provide a comfortable vantage point from which I can observe and stalk mice and moles, M&M's as I call them.

Out of desperation one day, I crawled under the garden shed for cooler shelter. Something had already done the digging to provide access. I had just nicely settled in when I spotted a mole scurrying towards the opening through which I had just entered. I lunged forward, and in my haste, left a bit of fur on the underside of a beam. Ignoring the pain, I exited in time to see a flash of grey and a blur of tiny legs scooting around the corner of the building. In hot pursuit and with a devil-may-care attitude, I reached the far side of the shed as the object of my attention disappeared under an overturned wheelbarrow. My feline instincts and past experience dictated that I should take the shorter route over the top and pounce as my prey exited from beneath. The element of surprise works every time … or so I thought!

As I sailed through the air, unable to change directions, I realized my folly. One large and four small black-and-white-striped critters were assembled directly beneath me … where I was about to land.

Minutes later, barely able to breathe, I dragged my putrid body towards Jenna who was working in a nearby flower bed. I had no idea what had just occurred but Jenna obviously recognized the distinctive odour and quickly backed away from me, a look of trepidation on her face. Reaching the house in record time, she quickly shut the door leaving me no option but to remain outside.

As I sat on the lawn in the heat of the noonday sun the odour intensified.

After what seemed to be a very long time, Jenna reappeared, barely recognizable, swaddled in plastic outerwear from head to toe, a large bucket of water in each hand. My first reaction was to bolt, but sanity prevailed and I followed her to a remote area of our property. Her return trip to the house produced cloths, towels, shampoo and an array of other substances I didn't recognize. I could tell that Jenna was not looking forward to the impending task any more than I was, although I wasn't quite sure just what was awaiting me.

Donning rubber gloves to complete the ensemble, Jenna lifted me into one of the buckets of water. My protests fell on deaf ears. Initially my face received the most attention. Fortunately none of the offending sticky substance had entered my eyes.

Once I was thoroughly wet, I was removed from the now foul-smelling water and a potion of some sort was rubbed in my fur. After a few minutes I was immersed in the second bucket of water. This process was repeated a few more times as more pails of water were brought from the house.

A final shampoo and towel-dry left me smelling rather nice and feeling refreshed. By late afternoon, the pails cleaned, towels discarded and having spent the better part of an hour in the shower, Jenna was confident that there was no lingering odour.

Wesley was first to arrive home from work shortly thereafter. His usual cheerful greeting resonated through the house as he entered. With Jenna not being in the immediate vicinity, his attention was focused on the family feline. As he lifted me from my basket to his shoulder he commented on my immaculate grooming and fresh scent.

Jenna entered the room a few minutes later with hair still damp and her smiling face shiny from a thorough scrubbing. As Wesley moved forward to greet her, a quizzical look shadowed his face and he inquired, "Have you been in close proximity to a skunk today?"

Upon hearing the details of my escapade, Wesley imparted some good advice for the future . . . "Look before you leap."

I do hope that you will be able to visit me sometime this summer.

Puurrrs,
Sugar

Sugar Visits The Big City

Dear Mom & Dad,

It was truly a pleasant surprise to see you recently. Family members were careful not to "let the cat out of the bag" regarding your impending visit. The unique scratching post you brought me is a work of art and remains a topic of conversation among visitors to our home. Who would have thought that genuine moleskin was available in so many different colours? I have only ever seen grey-skinned moles myself.

My propensity for being in the wrong place at the wrong time continues to be a source of anxiety for my adoptive family. The latest embarrassing sequence of events began to unfold one morning in early autumn.

I had been up as usual before daybreak with Jenna and Wesley. My grooming routine finally completed after my wholesome breakfast, I was about to settle in for a much-needed catnap. Jenna had already left for the day and Wesley was in and out of the house and garage preparing for his departure as well.

The anticipated peace and quiet of having the house all to myself was not yet a reality. The sound of noisy activity reverberated from the kitchen. I sauntered in and observed Jason preparing his breakfast, being ever so cautious not to have a mishap with his newly acquired business attire. My usual allotment of morning treats from him was not forthcoming and he seemed to be preoccupied. Feeling somewhat dejected, I followed Wesley to the garage and from atop Jason's car, I observed the procedures surrounding a tire change on the family Jeep.

My attention span is rather short when I am suffering from sleep deprivation so I gazed around for a suitable place to partake of my overdue nap. The back seat of Jason's car looked most inviting as I peered through the rear window. My luck held up as I was able to gain entry by skillfully manoeuvring my not-so-svelte body through a space left between the glass and the frame on the driver's side.

I was obviously exhausted not to have been aware of Wesley's departure, or the fact that I was now in a moving vehicle myself. I can't determine how long I slept, but according to Jason he was "past the point of no return" on his way to the city when my head appeared over his shoulder causing him to have a near accident, if not heart failure.

As he related the saga during the evening meal, he stated that the fright I gave him soon became the least of his concerns. He was en route to an interview for a much-sought-after job and returning home to deposit me at that point would have resulted in his late arrival. On the other hand ... what was he to do with me during the interview? Serious consequences could result from leaving a pet unattended in a vehicle on a warm day.

Already experiencing an elevated stress level, this new turn of events compounded his anxiety further. The absence of available parking in close proximity to his destination added to the dilemma as he navigated through slow-moving traffic in the city centre.

Sometime later, a parking spot found and the decision having been made, Jason donned his suit jacket, straightened his tie and lifted me out of the car. Making his way through the crowded streets he averted his eyes from curious onlookers.

As we journeyed on I became aware that it had been some time since I had used the facilities, as humans sometimes say, and my situation was becoming rather urgent. Jason being the intuitive person he is, sensed my need, I suppose in part due to the squirming of my body and my back claws piercing his thigh. With an inflection of pleading in his voice he encouraged me to "hang in there" while he re-routed through an open-air parking lot. Moments later I emerged from beneath a parked car much relieved.

Upon our arrival at the designated address, thankfully on time, the team of interviewers were somewhat taken aback, to say the least, by the sight of a prospective employee entering the boardroom with a large grey cat under his arm.

An explanation was obviously required and as the story unfolded prior to the commencement of the interview, staff members were commissioned to bring forth from the lunchroom whatever suitable feline fare was available, along with a dish of water and a bowl of milk. A cushion materialized from somewhere as well and after partaking of the generous offerings, I fell fast asleep.

The interview finally over, we made our way home. According to Jason there would no doubt be numerous graduates vying for the position he was seeking, and he expressed concern to Wesley and Jenna that the unfortunate events of the day could have detrimental repercussions.

The waiting period was nerve-racking for Jason and indeed the whole family. It was stressful for me as well since I felt totally responsible for the entire fiasco.

Mercifully, however, the goddesses of feline heaven were looking out for me. A week later Jason was notified that he was the successful applicant.

As Jason settled into his new job he found himself to be something of a celebrity around the water cooler and was asked repeatedly to recount the details of the now circulating, "cat in the boardroom" story.

Jason learned that although there were several young men and women who were equally qualified for the position, his decision to consider my safety, despite the possibility of jeopardizing his employment opportunity, was well received by the board members who were themselves caring pet owners.

Wesley summed it all up by saying, "All's well that ends well," and he confided to me that he too had had a few naps on the back seats of cars.

Love & Puurrrs,
Sugar

Halloween

HAPPY HALLOWEEN

Dear Mom & Dad,

We seem to be approaching that time of the year again when there are fewer daylight hours and the outdoor temperature has dropped below my comfort zone. On a positive note, gardening season is finally over so I am no longer burdened with guilt for not wanting to be outside every day with Jenna "enjoying the fresh air."

I did venture out one day last week, however, when my family members were decorating the front yard for an event called Halloween. This was a new experience for me so I was intrigued by the preparations that were being made.

Jason and Wesley had brought home bales of straw and several pumpkins in various sizes. Jenna carved humorous faces on the pumpkins and arranged them on the steps and along the walkway. Her people figures, which she made from straw, old clothes, scarves and hats, were positioned on wooden benches and accessorized with a few garden implements.

I enjoyed watching the activity as everyone worked at their specific tasks. Jason at one point set me on the ground in front of the straw figures and then took several pictures. My reward for cooperating, which was entirely out of character, was a few treats and a long-overdue tummy rub. You will no doubt be the recipients of a few of these rare photos.

I was not aware that there was more to Halloween than the above-mentioned decorations. I was definitely not prepared for what transpired at our house after dark a few nights later. My fur is still standing on end and Jason has remarked that "I'm as nervous as a cat." I suppose that does make sense . . . somehow!

My family had had an earlier-than-usual dinner that night so my dining schedule was also advanced. I had just finalized my grooming routine and was about to settle in for some quiet time when the doorbell rang. The house, with its open concept design, afforded me an unobstructed view of the entry from my basket. Jenna hurried to the door as if she was expecting someone. Curious to see who might be visiting, I glanced towards the open door.

I stared wide-eyed at what I saw! There stood what appeared to be an old woman holding a long stick, dressed entirely in black and wearing a large pointed hat. She also had a whopper of a nose that had a wart on the end of it. I have seen some scary cats in my day but never anything of that magnitude . . . perhaps humans have another level of ugly!

This wretched-looking person made some cackling noises and then whispered something to Jenna that sounded like a threat. Jenna showed no signs of fear but instead gave the old woman some treats she had on hand and the woman disappeared into the darkness.

Before Jenna could close the door two more strange creatures came around the corner of the house. One was small and white with two round eyes and no arms or legs that I could see. Trailing close behind was a long-tailed beast covered in green scales. Its front legs, which were off the ground and flapping in the air, appeared more like human arms and hands. By now I was out of my basket and hiding under Wesley's chair in the kitchen. I couldn't hear what was being said but I presume that they too made threats since Jenna gave them something as well and they quickly scurried away.

The doorbell rang many more times that evening and from the safety of my hiding place I observed the strangest sights. I had no idea that rabbits could grow to be that large, nor had I ever seen a mouse with such big ears and walking on its hind legs.

I think a few humans came to the door also. I just hope that they didn't encounter the old lady or the beasts.

The doorbell finally fell silent but it took a bowl of warm milk and my basket moved into Wesley's closet before I could finally fall asleep. I shudder to think what would have happened if Jenna did not have candy to give those menacing creatures.

I hope that you didn't have any such experience at your house.

Puurrrs,
Sugar

Grey Cup

NO
CAT
ZONE

Dear Mom & Dad,

Humans seem to use different phrases to describe the period of time referred to as a "week" such as, the beginning of the week, midweek and the weekend. I make no such distinctions, except that out-of-town house guests seem to arrive on the days called the weekend.

I rather like when people visit our home as I am usually fussed over, and my silver and grey tabby markings always bring forth a barrage of flattering comments.

Unfortunately, my family had a house guest this past weekend that was the exception to the above rule. Jenna's Uncle Nigel was here from England on a business venture and his new wife Beatrice had accompanied him. Beatrice seemed pleasant enough until I made my entrance into the room. She backed away from me and declared that she did not like cats! She claimed that being in close proximity to felines makes her sneeze and have a runny nose. “Rubbish!” said Uncle Nigel. “I have never heard of anyone from England not liking cats . . . regardless of any allergies they may have.” She punctuated his remark with another sneeze!

“Aunt Bea,” I soon discovered, was also the culprit responsible for the guest room being declared a NO CAT ZONE. Family members tried very hard to keep me as far from her as possible, but I am afraid that my lingering presence has been well distributed throughout the house.

Saturday was peaceful, since everyone was away for most of the day and I once again had the run of the house, as Wesley calls my unrestricted movements when I am home alone.

Sunday, however, was a different matter. By midafternoon all activities and dialogue seemed to revolve around watching something called The Grey Cup. Food items were prepared in advance so that there would be no disruptions once the viewing began.

This viewing was to encompass a time period of about three hours, or so I surmised from their conversation as I listened from an adjoining room.

Eventually, the *telly* was turned on, as Uncle Nigel calls the television, and everyone quickly settled in the family room — except me of course! I wasn't allowed in because of "you know who."

The euphemism "there is more than one way to skin a cat" came to mind (it definitely wasn't a cat who thought up that terminology) and I plotted my strategy. When no one was looking I snuck behind the sofa on which Aunt Bea was sitting and I settled myself in for the afternoon.

Whatever was being watched was now being referred to as "the game" but I was not any more enlightened than when it was being called The Grey Cup.

I did manage to stay awake for the beginning of the event, which seemed to get off to a bad start. The spectators in attendance were noisy and appeared to be getting increasingly restless as they waited. Finally, dozens of very large men came running onto a field and the shouting escalated. I presumed they were late arriving and that is what all of the fuss was about.

When the action finally got under way, the participants seemed not to be getting on well with each other. A great deal of pushing and shoving was taking place. I was particularly confused by the brown-coloured object called "the ball" that was being thrown around. It seemed to be a much-coveted item but when one of the men caught it he either dropped it or quickly threw it away.

Uncle Nigel took the opportunity to inform everyone that the game of football originated in his homeland in the nineteenth century or earlier. Apparently, back in the day, the original ball with which the game was played was called a "pigskin" since it was made from a pig's inflated bladder. He added that it sometimes had to be blown up several times by the players in the course of a game — hence the introduction of leather and rubber spheres, which were more palatable to the senses. This bit of historical insight seemed to discourage further interest in the pâté de foie platter.

Mercifully I catnapped through most of the activity. I was awakened, albeit prematurely, by the sound of sneezing and nose blowing. By this time Aunt Bea had gone through a whole box of tissues and was asking Jenna for more. (Tee-hee!)

I made a valiant effort to understand the concept of this "sport" but it was an exercise in futility. I will never understand how humans can be enthralled by such boring drivel. Now, a bunch of cats chasing a mouse — that is what I call real entertainment! I would definitely be up for watching three hours of a game called The Grey Mouse.

Puurrrs,
Sugar

’O Sole Mio

NEW
TEMPTING TUNA
KITTY COOKIES!
CAT TREATS
with Tartar Control

Dear Mom & Dad,

I hope that you had a nice Christmas with your guests from Hawaii. A white Christmas would surely be a new experience for them. Thank you for the gifts. The cat calendar is right up my alley.

I enjoyed the excitement of the season and all of the extra attention bestowed on me by friends and family who came to our home during the holidays. As usual I was spoiled with gifts and goodies. I have gained a bit of weight thanks in part to the several packages of feline treats you included in my Christmas package. I especially like the *Tempting Tuna* flavour with tartar control. The latter, according to

Jenna, is beneficial in maintaining fresh breath and a winning smile.

I tested this premise one day when I was home alone and I had "accidentally" knocked over one of the packages of treats, which had been left open and was barely secured between cans of cat food in the back of the cupboard. This mishap was a blessing in disguise, as I had been feeling the onset of serious tartar buildup, and I therefore took the opportunity to indulge myself. By the time I had finished the last morsel, however, any smile I might have had, winning or otherwise, was not forthcoming due to a terrible tummy ache.

Jason was first to discover the evidence of my folly, and although he is usually my co-conspirator, he spilled the beans to Jenna when she noticed that I wasn't quite myself, and I did not have my usual appetite for my evening meal.

As the holiday season comes to an end, there is one positive aspect of it being over — I will not have to listen to *Jingle Bells* (and the six different versions of it) for another year. My family leave the radio on to "keep me company" when everyone is away during the day, but I suspect that it is more likely left on to deter prospective burglars, since my guard-cat skills are all but non-existent.

On one such day, shortly after Christmas, the house quiet except for the radio, I was napping peacefully when I was awakened to what sounded like rodents singing! *Rodents singing?* I thought I was dreaming until I heard a voice announcing that the song was sung by Alvin and the Chipmunks! *Chipmunks?* Well, that gave me an idea! If chipmunks can sing, why not cats? With a burst of enthusiasm I decided to work on a few lyrics to surprise Wesley and Jenna when they returned home from shopping.

With New Year's Eve approaching, I thought of impressing them with a few bars of "Auld Lang Syne" but I very quickly determined that something the like of "'O Sole Mio" was more suited to feline vocal cords. After a couple of hours of practice I felt certain that I had genuine potential and I envisioned a screaming crowd as I made my debut appearance on the new TV show, *Fabulous Felines*. Perhaps I would even take home the coveted Golden Whisker Award for best new talent.

My reverie was interrupted when I heard Jenna and Wesley open the front door. My heart pounding with excitement, I cleared my throat, took a deep breath and belted out "Ohoooooo Sooole Mi . . . !" I didn't quite get Mioooo out when I heard the clatter of bags hitting the floor as Wesley bound up the steps two at a time, Jenna close behind. I was actually quite startled as I didn't know what had provoked their reaction. I looked up at them quizzically as they stood over me, their eyes wide with fear and concern.

After Wesley did a thorough examination of my entire body, by which he determined that I had not been shot, Jenna offered the suggestion that I may have been attempting to dislodge a furball. My ego by now was totally shattered and my illusion of a singing career destroyed forever. Matters were made even worse when Jason arrived home and upon hearing the details of the mysterious "wailing noises" hypothesized that I may have once again overindulged in the tartar-control treats and I was experiencing another stomach ache.

Perhaps I should have selected a more traditional song such as *Silent Mice.*

Puurrrs,
Sugar

Home Alone

Dear Mom & Dad,

This is just a short note to let you know that I am on my way to the Bulrush Boarding Kennel for a couple of days.

When I heard my family discussing arrangements for my stay at the kennel, I tried very hard to appear responsible by being on my best behaviour for the next few days. I had hoped that they would reconsider and leave me at home, as they did on a previous occasion ... with bowls of food, treats, my choice of beds, chairs and sofas to sleep on, and of course the requisite new toy resembling a mouse — green with an orange tail and yellow ears!

Regrettably their mistrust may be somewhat justified. Last summer they allowed me to stay alone for a day and a night and when they returned Jason said it looked like "hell had broken loose" in the house.

I must admit that I had some reckless moments during the twenty-four hours in which I had the house all to myself. My hyperactivity was no doubt attributable to the fact that I began wolfing down the open package of treats as soon as the last suitcase went out the door and Wesley had engaged the Home Monitoring System. A moment of panic occurred when I realized that the HMS was another name for a *burglar alarm*. I had not thought of what I might do if confronted with a burglar, or worse still, one of those creatures that came to our door on the night called Halloween.

Normally the treats are doled out rather frugally by Jenna, her rationale being that if animals are given too many treats at one time they become hyper, much like children do when given too much candy. I have never suffered greatly from the enforcement of that theory since I can usually count on a few extra morsels from Wesley or Jason when Jenna isn't looking. Of course some caution must be taken by them so as not to deplete the bag too quickly or the discrepancy would certainly be noticed. Anyhow, after consuming the whole package of *Saveur d'oiseau* morsels that had a distinct hummingbird aftertaste, I could feel the onset of a "hell breaking loose" sensation overtaking my body. YIKES! Jenna's theory was right!

The draperies provoked a challenge which could only be subdued by a view of the living room from atop the horizontal curtain rods. Satisfied that I still had the agility of a more youthful me, I then overturned a few flower pots. I have always found rolling in soft earth to be somewhat therapeutic so I indulged myself. Feeling ready for a nap, the nearest white chair called to me.

When I awoke night was approaching and my dinner was waiting, in the form of dried pellets. Wesley was adamant that my usual repast of Sea Creature Gumbo would not meet safety standards if left out at room temperature. Believe me, those pellets do not leave the palate craving for more, but Jenna insists they are nutritious — chock full of vitamins and minerals specifically formulated for cats, plus an ingredient for furball control, another for good bladder function and yet another for my peripheral vision.

She would be very upset if she knew that I occasionally supplement my diet with a fresh mole or mouse. I remember Granddaddy Pudster telling us kittens that he drank milk and ate mice all his life. He lived to be seventeen years old. I rest my case!

I will write again soon and let you know about my weekend at Bulrush. I hope the kennel is not too boring!

Puurrrs,
Sugar

Adventures At The Bulrush Boarding Kennel

BULRUSH BOARDING KENNEL
OPEN
the
CAT'S meow
the
BARKER'S BARRACKS

Dear Mom & Dad,

As you will recall, in my last letter I was expressing great resistance to my upcoming sojourn at the kennel, having anticipated two days of ear-scratching, paw-licking boredom. Much to my surprise, however, it was quite an eventful experience.

I am ashamed to say, therefore, that I behaved rather badly when it was time to leave for the kennel. At first sight of the transportation vehicle, I slunk off to my only bastion as yet undiscovered by family members. Unfortunately, in my haste I neglected to retract my tail as I hid behind the towels in the linen closet. My oversight was eventually detected by Wesley as he approached the area of the closet for the fourth time, a somewhat urgent tone discernible in his voice as he called my name. Although time was now an issue, he patiently attempted (repeatedly) to extract me from the back of the closet as I maintained the classic *flat cat* crouching position. Eventually succeeding in his efforts, I emerged with back claws firmly gripping a large pink bath towel.

Suffice to say, we arrived at the kennel considerably later than the pre-arranged check-in time. "Due to unforeseen circumstances," said Jenna, without elaborating.

After the necessary documentation was attended to, my belligerence still intact, I had to be encouraged to leave my carry cage and even more persuasion was required to get me into the large, see-through, metal-bar enclosure that would be my dwelling for the next couple of days. I was pleasantly surprised, however, to see that some comforts of home had accompanied me. There awaiting my arrival was my sleeping basket, complete with my paw-print blanket and, unless the kennel coincidently possessed like-patterned dishes to mine, I also had my own fish-motif bowls for food and water.

My primary concern as I looked about was the possibility that I would have to share a communal commode. As you know I am rather sensitive about that sort of thing. Fortunately, my anxiety was premature, as in came Wesley carrying my portable that had been cleaned and restocked with fresh-scent, super-clumping, dust-free, soft-on-the-paws litter. I must admit that I would forego this man-made concoction any day for the comfort provided by the soft earth in a freshly planted flower garden.

I nevertheless felt lonely for a few hours until two more cats were brought in by their owner and put in the enclosure adjacent to mine. They actually seemed happy to be there and I determined that it was not their first time at Bulrush. They "meowed me up" straight away (that's cat lingo for chatted me up) and I learned that their names were Shenanigan and Kai-Bosh. I was soon to find out that they had been appropriately named by their human. When I could get a meow in edgewise, I inquired as to where they were from. I was surprised to discover that our families live quite near each other, our respective homes separated only by a small wooded area.

Shenanigan and Kai-Bosh were quite eager to familiarize me with life at Bulrush. I quickly learned that there were other animals in the kennel besides cats. That news brought on a hair-rising sensation until it was pointed out that we were in the section called the Cat's Meow which is separate from the dog compound aptly named the Barker's Barracks. Someone obviously has a sense of humour. I expect that there is a "Hamster Haven," "Rabbit Run" and perhaps even a "Mouse House" somewhere on the premises.

I was also informed that the facility is owned and operated by a woman named Veronika — a name that no four-legged resident could pronounce — so she is known to all as "Missie."

My first encounter with Missie was when she came in to inquire about my diet and feeding schedule before my family departed. There are times when I would dearly love to speak human words such as, "Just leave ample food in my dish at all times and I will decide when I want to eat!" and "Please, none of those nutritional pellets!" As was the case, we all got fed at the same time regardless of any notations Missie had written on our respective charts.

The main office and check-in counter, where all of the animals arrive and depart from, is adjacent to the Cat's Meow, therefore no guests come or go without being scrutinized by the felines in residence.

As night was approaching, a family arrived with what I initially thought was a small horse or perhaps a bear, but was actually a dog of enormous proportions. His tongue, which was hanging out the side of his mouth over a rail of inch-long teeth, appeared to be half the size of my body. I learned that his name was Bogart and he was a Newfoundland breed of dog. I inquired as to how far down the corridor the Barker's Barracks was located, and I determined that the distance was not sufficient for my liking.

After Missie had seemingly left for the night and I had a tasteless meal of an unidentified substance (those pellets might not be so bad after all), Shenanigan and Kai-Bosh seemed to be in conference about something, their tails swishing and ears flicking. Up until now the kennel had been rather quiet and I was looking forward to a nap. Suddenly, Kai-Bosh opened his mouth and a meowel came forth that could dislodge a digested hairball from any cat within hearing distance. As I emerged cautiously from under my blanket, one ear at a time, my fur standing on end, the Barker's Barracks erupted in a chorus of yips, yelps and a baritone bark that no doubt belonged to Bogart.

I didn't know that cats could laugh but Shenanigan and Kai-Bosh were engaged in something akin to human laughter as they rolled around on the floor of their enclosure. At that moment the kennel door flew open and in came Missie. A dash to the Barracks and subsequent investigation did not shed any light on what caused the commotion. Satisfied that there was no threat to any of the furry residents in other quarters, Missie had a quick look in our compound only to find me still peeking out from under my blanket and Shenanigan and Kai-Bosh possessing looks of innocence that would make angels appear guilty.

Day 2 . . .

Despite having my own basket and blanket, I slept poorly. I was missing my family and the familiar surroundings of home.

When my breakfast arrived, seemingly at the crack of dawn, I had just fallen back to sleep and was enjoying a dream that involved fresh morsels of mouse. My sleep interrupted, I looked over to see if my kennel mates were awake as well, only to discover that something was amiss. Neither had eaten the contents of their food bowls and Shenanigan was lying on her back, eyes closed, with all four paws in the air. Kai-Bosh appeared to be trying to regurgitate something from the back of his throat. My initial concern quickly turned to fear and then went into paranoia overdrive as I considered the possibility that their conditions were due to the previous night's ghastly repast, of which I had partaken, albeit, very little. The power of suggestion brought on a sudden attack of "je ne sais quoi" which had me dashing for my fresh-scent, super-clumping, dust-free, soft-on-the-paws litter. With the possibility of another traumatic situation developing, Missie once again came rushing in. Kai-Bosh's guttural hacking noises had now escalated considerably. With a face ashen with fear, Missie quickly entered their enclosure and began to examine Shenanigan who appeared to be in a catatonic state. Kai-Bosh, out of breath I suspect, slumped to the floor. Missie, in a state that could only be described as panic mode, sprinted to her office simultaneously speed-dialing for help as the situation was clearly in need of professional assistance.

Shortly thereafter a young man came bounding in with instruments already in hand, one of which I immediately recognized. I am of the belief that no feline ailment can be determined without the use of the dreaded thermometer.

After a thorough examination of Shenanigan, who was now responding to human attention, the diagnosis was "possible intestinal sensitivity due to the consumption of unfamiliar and indigestible food." Likewise was the conclusion from the thermometer reading on Kai-Bosh, since there appeared to be no other logical explanation.

The young veterinarian eventually departed having recommended a menu change for my fellow felines consisting of nothing but freshly caught fish, deboned of course, or cooked poultry, likewise bone free. Either choice was to be chopped into small bits and served at room temperature every three hours.

A short time later, gazing at my still uneaten breakfast while Missie delivered the freshly caught fish, fishing pole still in hand, I wondered if perhaps I should have consumed more of my dinner. Clearly a "touch of intestinal sensitivity" had benefits.

Noting the speed and enthusiasm with which Shenanigan and Kai-Bosh were devouring their first meal, after what seemed like their near-death experiences, I had the distinct feeling that their recovery was not as miraculous as I had first thought. Missie had no doubt fallen prey to another of their well-orchestrated capers. A wink and a Cheshire grin from Kai-Bosh, as he licked a morsel of trout from the side of his mouth, confirmed my suspicions.

The remainder of the day was uneventful by comparison and when my family came for me, thankfully before dinner, I went peacefully into my carry cage for the ride home.

Love & Puurrrs,
Sugar

A Dog Named Chesapeake

Dear Mom & Dad,

I am not sure what human word would best describe my current emotional state, but I think *frazzled* would probably be accurate. I overheard Jenna use the term to describe herself to a friend, and I think it is safe to say that everyone in the household is feeling much the same way.

Our once quiet home is now housing a dog named Chesapeake, who is anything but quiet. He has, thus far, only been with us for a week, but from a cat's perspective any amount of time is too long to be in the company of such a rambunctious young dog.

Chesapeake belongs to Wesley's father, Jordan, who recently became ill and has been hospitalized.

Wesley and Jenna agreed to look after his dog until such time as he is home and recovered. I was not consulted on this decision.

Chess, as he is sometimes called, is six months old and still in puppy mode. He was recently neutered as well, and arrived wearing an e-collar around his head and neck to prevent him from compromising the surgical area. I have to sympathize with him in that regard as I have vivid memories of having to wear that ridiculous contraption myself, which makes many simple tasks all but impossible to navigate.

I waited patiently for hours, gazing out the front window on the day Wesley was to arrive with his cargo. I had no idea what size of dog was about to invade my space but I was hoping he would be considerably smaller than Bogart. My fears were not assuaged when I saw the size of his transportation vehicle in the back of the family Jeep.

Wesley, not being accustomed to young canine behaviour, neglected to attach the leash to Chesapeake's collar upon releasing him from his enclosure. As soon as freedom was evident Chess bolted towards the road directing a frantic bark at a passing car — Wesley in hot pursuit.

The leash now firmly secured, Chesapeake arrived at the front door with Wesley in tow. Jenna was in the lower level of the house preparing a corner of the utility room for Chesapeake's sleeping quarters and didn't realize that the "guest" had arrived. Hearing the lock disengage on the door, she sprinted upstairs but was too late to whisk me out of sight.

As the door opened and Chesapeake's head thrust forward straining against the leash, I assumed full combat mode — my back up, tail fluffed, claws at the ready — and I emitted my most fearsome hiss inches from his face. I wanted to establish straight away that this was my territory and I was not going to be intimidated. Within seconds, however, I knew I had taken the wrong approach. My full height barely reached Chesapeake's knees and when he gave me a friendly *woof* his breath parted the fur on top of my head and a fine spray of his saliva settled on my whiskers. I did not resist when Jenna relocated me to another room and closed the door.

As my family quickly realized, the house had not been dog-proofed. A swipe of Chesapeake's tail knocked over the decorative vase at the entry. Wesley made a valiant but futile effort to grab it before it made contact with the tiled floor. The noise of the vase breaking caused Chess to again bolt and the leash disengaged from Wesley's hand. A quick reconnaissance around the main living area of the house brought down a free-standing rack of CDs when the leash tangled around its base. Jenna finally cornered the canine in the computer room and was all but knocked over backwards by the weight of a large paw on each of her shoulders accompanied by a swipe of dog tongue from chin to forehead by way of a greeting.

Jason was quickly commissioned by Wesley and Jenna to take Chesapeake for a (long) walk while they came up with a viable arrangement by which to live somewhat peacefully with twenty kilos of untamed energy, for a period of time yet to be determined.

The outdoor temperature, still below freezing, dictated that Chess be kept inside the house. It was also decided that it would not be fair to confine him to one room for the duration of his stay with us. Chesapeake was accustomed to roaming freely outdoors on a large country property and seemingly had a great deal of freedom while indoors as well. All things considered, and given his young age and energy level, Wesley and Jenna made the decision to accommodate their guest by rearranging the furniture and decor.

Large items of furniture were covered with blankets and sheets and pushed against the walls. Lamps were aligned atop cabinets. Small items were likewise placed out of reach of the wagging tail and saucer-sized paws. Indoor plants, of which we have many, were assembled in the guest room with the door closed.

Confident that the dog-proofing was complete, Jason was allowed to return with his charge. Everyone had assumed that the outing would have tired Chesapeake . . . at least temporarily. That was not to be. As the door opened, large snow-covered paws danced across the hardwood floors; their owner, confused by the new look of his surroundings, decided that another tour of the entire house was in order. Having been released from my "holding cell" while Chess was being walked, I now relocated from the fireplace mantle to safety atop the tallest kitchen cupboard. In the meantime several large towels were placed strategically at the entry.

Chess eventually made his way to the kitchen where he found my eating area. His large tongue lapped at my water bowl and he "smiled" up at me as liquid dripped from his open mouth. At this point Wesley decided to bring Chess's belongings in from the Jeep. I was in awe of the size of his water and food bowls. His bag of puppy kibbles required Jason's assistance to be carried into the house. Lastly, Chesapeake's toys made their entrance. Most of the saliva-covered items were the size of my body, or larger, and his chew bone had to have once belonged to a dinosaur.

Needless to say, I want Wesley's father to recover from his illness as quickly as possible, but I found myself emphasizing the *quickly* as I gazed around at the disarray of our once orderly home.

Bedtime brought on new challenges for my already weary family. The spacious utility room had been converted into a temporary guest room for Chesapeake, his doggie bed installed with toys and water bowl in close proximity. The door was closed to prevent Chess from roaming during the night.

The house now quiet, I finally descended from my lofty perch and was heading for my sleeping quarters, via my food bowl, when I heard what sounded like a duck squawk emitting from somewhere in the house. I heard it several more times before Jason emerged from his room with a puzzled look on his face. A few more squawks brought forth two more sleepy-eyed figures. Jason being the most recent family member (although some years ago) to have played with a squeaky toy, recognized the sound for what it was. A descent by all into the lower level confirmed that the mystery sound was indeed produced by one of Chesapeake's toys as he flung it around the room.

The rubber duck, wrestled from Chess's jaws, was placed outside the utility room and everyone returned to bed. The peace was short-lived. Chess began to howl and scratch at the closed door. Shortly thereafter, each family member arrived back downstairs bearing an item to hopefully pacify the young canine. Wesley contributed an old T-shirt tied in a knot in lieu of a toy, Jenna offered a dog biscuit and Jason produced a snack of kibbles. All was again peaceful although Chess showed no interest in the offerings. The night-clad figures had not reached their respective beds when the howling started again, and this time it was accompanied by a bark. It was evident that Chess did not want to be alone.

Midnight now approaching, Jason concluded that if he, or anyone else, were to get any sleep, he would have to spend the night in the utility room with Chess. An air mattress and sleeping bag were brought forth from storage and set up near Chesapeake's doggie bed. The house finally tranquil, everyone fell into a deep sleep.

Jason has had to be Chesapeake's night companion all week. He attempted to slip out of the utility room and back to his own bed one night but Chess was not to be fooled, and we all had to endure another round of barking and howling until Jason once again tucked into his sleeping bag between the clothes dryer and Chess's bed. Needless to say, the rest of the household is thankful for Jason's very selfless act.

Jenna's daytime activities revolve around Chesapeake's needs. Due to the proximity of the road to our house, he cannot be left to roam freely outdoors, however he does need a great deal of exercise and play time. Jenna has become proficient at stick throwing and as her throwing distance improves, she envisions it one day becoming an Olympic event.

As of this writing Wesley's father is still unable to resume caring for Chesapeake. I will keep you abreast of ongoing activities in my next letter.

Puurrrs,
Sugar

Cuda Writes To Sugar

refresh
artesian spring water
refresh
spring water
refresh
artesian spring wa

Dear Sugar,

Even though we have never met, it is good to know that somewhere, far away in Eastern Canada I have a cousin. I occasionally need a fellow feline to meow to who understands life from a cat's perspective. I do hope that we can be friends and correspond from time to time.

As you do, I live with a human family. I have been with Peter and Heidi since I was a kitten and I have always been well cared for — truth be known, they spoil me rotten. I am tempted to refer to them as Mama and Papa, as does their daughter Anna when she visits, but that might cause confusion since I bear no resemblance to either of them — just a little cat humour dear cousin!

I heard a great deal about you after Peter and Heidi returned from visiting your family last summer. Our families are related somehow but as yet, the exact lineage eludes me. Heidi says she and Jenna are "ex-cousins-in-law." She then laughs and says that this genealogical category is not yet defined in the dictionary. So, let's you and I just be cousins?

My family moves quite frequently because of Peter's specialized field of work. We have just recently relocated to a place so far north in Alberta that it is said that Santa has a workshop here. As I age, it becomes harder and harder for me to adjust to new surroundings. If I never see another suitcase in my life, it will be too soon.

Before we came up here Heidi and Peter went on what they call a holiday. They couldn't take me with them, so I was left with friends of theirs for what seemed like quite a long time. The humans were very kind to me but they have a cat of their own named Lester and he didn't like me. He hissed and lunged at me at every opportunity. He even pulled out some of my fur when no one was looking. Under my breath I called him "Lester the Pester."

Their holiday over, my family finally came to pick me up and for a few days I enjoyed being back in the familiar surroundings of our condominium, which seems to be their home base between assignments. The comfort was short-lived, however, as there was a flurry of activity one morning and out came suitcases and moving boxes. Two days later I was in my travel cage on the back seat of their SUV wedged between Peter's prized Yamaha keyboard and Heidi's house plants, one of which is a palm that has grown to be a substantial size. My travel cage is usually positioned high enough so that I am able to see outside when I am awake but the palm was definitely a problem on the last trip, as was the spider plant, which seems to have sprouted a profusion of offshoots recently. As a result, my field of vision was obscured to the point that I felt like I was travelling through the rain forest. Fortunately, I slept a great deal en route as the hum of the engine and gentle movement of the car were somewhat soothing.

Normally the voyages involve stopping over at places they call Hotels and Lodges along the way. On the most recent occasion, my family stopped for the night after a long drive, only to discover that the Lodge they had chosen had a no-pet policy.

Let me tell you, I was not a happy camper when I heard that. How insulting! I happen to be a very responsible cat. I do not create noise, drop food on the floor, or use anything but my designated litter box for my needs. And I definitely would not leave with their towels in my travel cage. No amount of praise for my impeccable behaviour, however, would convince the proprietors to make an exception to the rule — just this once. So on we went in search of a more cat-friendly place to stay. A rather nasty snowstorm was developing which did not help matters, or moods.

There seemed to be a lot of desolate area between towns as we travelled north, but eventually Peter expressed relief that there were lights in the distance and I distinctly heard him whisper, "Please let there be pet-friendly accommodations in this town."

Fortunately, they were in luck. My family was welcomed, as was I, at a Motel called VACANCY, the sign so brightly lit that Heidi spotted it from two kilometres away.

I am still confused by the different names of places where we stay. Sometimes we spend the night at a Hotel or a Lodge, other times we are at a Motel or Inn, and most puzzling of all is a Bed and Breakfast.

They all look much the same to me from my vantage point at floor level.

Having had a good night's sleep and my favourite breakfast of Turkey Tongue Tidbits in Gravy (I didn't know that turkeys had tongues, did you?) I was prepared for what I understood to be the last leg of the trip. Pit stops were made regularly so that I could stretch my legs and attend to other matters.

Finally, we arrived at a place where there were more lights and vehicles than I had seen since leaving Calgary. I hoped that it was our final destination as my usual good nature was wearing thin. As Peter parked the SUV in front of a four-storey building, I heard two sighs in unison from the front seat. I knew we had arrived!

I was first to be unloaded; my cage was draped with a cover due to the cold temperature. Something seemed familiar, the smell of oil in the air perhaps. Now inside, my cover removed, we entered a small room. The doors closed and the whole room started to move upward. When it stopped the doors opened and we were in a new location. What a strange sensation! Once we were through another door I was let out of my confinement and Heidi said, "Welcome to your new home Cuda!"

That experience was a week ago. I have now settled in and become accustomed to all the new smells in the apartment. It is still too cold to be outdoors, but Peter says even when the weather is warmer I can't go out alone because there are wild animals in the area that could harm me. My thinking is ... what could be worse than Lester the Pester?

One, if not the most unsettling thing about my family living in so many different places is the difficulty I have in adjusting to the taste of the water. It may taste basically the same to humans, but we animals have a very keen sense of smell and taste — as you would know. At home in Calgary, we have a special filtering device under the sink so that the water we drink doesn't smell and taste like the contents of a swimming pool. With this in mind Heidi bought a supply of bottled water for Peter to take in his lunch and also for me to drink until I became accustomed to the tap water.

Anyhow, one day I had worked up a thirst after a rather strenuous workout tossing a "mouse" around the living room. (Our humans think that we are colour-blind, but I don't know of any self-respecting cat that could be fooled by a fluorescent orange thing with beady purple eyes, yellow ears and a bright green tail.) As I approached my water bowl I noticed a distinct odour that I could not identify. I can recall some pretty nasty tap water aromas but this was somehow different and I was reluctant to drink. I later made another attempt at quenching my thirst but the same odour was lingering. Now parched, I jumped up on the kitchen counter in search of tap water, rationalizing that it couldn't be any worse than what was in my bowl. My timing was off, however, and as I was about to lap up a few drops of water from the sink Heidi entered the room and proceeded to scold me for being on the counter where she prepares food. I slunk off to the bathroom only to find that the toilet seat was down (Peter was at work). I then looked longingly at the bathtub spout and found not a drop of moisture escaping. Where are those leaky faucets when you need them?

This scenario was repeated again the following day (with much more urgency) until Peter came home and casually mentioned to Heidi that he would prefer plain bottled water in his lunch rather than the flavoured varieties she had been providing. Heidi looked at me, then at my bowl and realization spread across her face; my odd behaviour was justified instantly.

Now, feeling badly about her oversight, Heidi has been wining and dining me ever since. In feline terms that means bowls of Deep Artesian Water in every room, pre-tasted personally by her, saucers of milk — the kind that is specifically formulated for feline consumption, and of course all the Turkey Tongue Tidbits I want.

One day I heard Peter wondering aloud why he was not receiving the same consideration and treatment as "the cat" since he was subjected to the flavoured water as well. Heidi smiled at him and replied that he was welcome to all the cat milk and Artesian Water he wanted but he probably would not like the Turkey Tongue Tidbits!

I hope I have not bored you with my saga, dear cousin. I look forward to hearing from you.

Puurrrs from Alberta,
Cuda

Sugar Writes to Cuda

Dear Cuda,

I was pleasantly surprised to receive your recent letter. I have known about you for some time and I have, in fact, seen photographs of you. Your distinct colouring and markings classify you as a "Tuxedo Cat," a rather elite group I am told.

I am sorry to learn of your travelling/relocating dilemmas. I can't equate, but I can sympathize. I am very much a homebody and thankfully, since coming to live with my present family, there have been few requirements for me to leave the premises. An occasional trip to see my veterinarian or to the boarding kennel is about the extent of my travels, and both are located a short distance from where we live.

I am approaching middle age, by human definition, and I have become rather set in my ways. I don't readily accept changes to my daily routine, although seasonal factors do have a bearing. During the winter months, which I prefer to categorize as the *lean cuisine months*, I mostly sleep, gaze longingly out the windows, and partake of whatever is put in my food bowl. The extent of my physical activity is to occasionally chase a "mouse" (mine being green fluorescent with a bell on its tail) around the house to keep my hunting skills from eroding during the off-season.

When the weather warms to an acceptable temperature, I miraculously have renewed energy and I prefer to be out and about, decimating the rodent population. This bit of information is to be kept strictly between us cats of course, as Jenna thinks that I consume only the well-balanced fare that she prepares for me, based on a mathematical formula factorizing my age, weight and activity level.

I too must be accompanied when I am outdoors as our property is in a wooded area and wild animals have been seen in the vicinity. Wesley has remarked that our property, if fenced, could be a wildlife sanctuary. Deer, foxes, raccoons, skunks, minks, rabbits, porcupines and coyotes are some of the species that frequent our yard. Bears have been known to venture into the area but, thus far, none have been seen by any family member. Jenna, however, suffered near heart failure last summer upon seeing our neighbour's large black dog emerging from the underbrush as she was watering plants early one morning. She claims that there is no distinction between the emotional impact of thinking one sees a bear and actually seeing one.

The above-mentioned animals are in abundance due in part to a designated Fauna and Flora Conservation Area in close proximity to our home. While my family would not harm any of the animals that venture into our backyard, Jenna does have to be creative in her efforts to minimize the destruction they cause to flowers, plants and shrubs. She long ago gave up her quest to maintain a vegetable garden, which had become a virtual smorgasbord for critters at harvest time.

Each of the *herbivorous predators*, as Jenna has "affectionately" named them, seems to have a different preference of domestic plant with which to supplement their diet. Deer, for example, enjoy the tasty leaves of the hosta plants that flourish in the more shaded areas of our backyard. One morning it was evident that several hostas had succumbed to a predator. Hoof prints in the vicinity of the dearly departed identified the culprit(s). Assuming that it was only a matter of time before the remaining plants would meet the same fate, Jenna purchased a repellent with which to spray what was left of the hosta population. The repellent is not harmful to animals but it has a bitter enough taste, supposedly, to encourage the herbivores to seek more palatable fare elsewhere.

Much to Jenna's dismay, however, the following morning not a hosta remained, save for a couple of roots, which had been disinterred and were lying shrivelled on the ground. I happened to be outdoors when this discovery was made and I quickly moved to safer ground, in the event that garden tools might take flight in all directions. To my surprise Jenna began to laugh. I later heard her relate the sequence of events to Wesley and they both concluded that the repellent was most likely perceived as salad dressing by the deer.

I have perhaps over-expounded somewhat on the subject of the outdoors, but with some fifteen or more gardens to care for plus two ponds and enough lawn area to host a Royal Wedding, my family is required to spend a great deal of time outdoors from April to October, and therefore I do as well.

I would like to clarify at this time that I don't live with my original human family as you do. Not so long ago, when my future was uncertain, I was put in the care of a very loving couple I now refer to as "Mom and Dad." They would have liked very much to have kept me, but at the time they were frequently away from home for extended periods of time and felt it would be unfair to subject me to the trauma of moving about and living with strangers during their absence. Instead, they found me a happy and stable home with Wesley, Jenna and Jason, for which I am grateful.

In closing, I would like to comment on how intrigued I was by your account of the flavoured water fiasco. I had no idea that water came in different flavours. I also quite like the sound of the Turkey Tongue Tidbits, but how do I relay to my family that I would like to try that variety of canned food? Any attempt to impart Turkey Tongue Tidbits by way of paw signals and facial expressions would surely initiate a hasty trip to the veterinarian — my family fearing the onset of a seizure.

I wish you well in your new location, Cuda. It is indeed nice to share feline thoughts with you. I look forward to your next letter.

Puurrrs,
Sugar

The Tooth

Dear Mom & Dad,

Since my last letter to you in late winter, peace and quiet has been restored in our home. Wesley's father made a complete recovery and Chesapeake has now been returned to him. Jason is adjusting well to sleeping in his own bed again.

Our furnishings had barely been put back in their original location when Uncle Nigel arrived unexpectedly from "Jolly Old"— as he calls his homeland. "That would be England," said Jenna as she delighted in translating his unfamiliar words for the rest of the family. Fortunately for me, Aunt Bea could not accompany him on this occasion. I had not been feeling well and being confined to one room, as I was for most of her previous visit, would not have enhanced my mood.

My tooth was becoming increasingly painful but I could not communicate that to my family. Jason was the first to suspect that something was dreadfully wrong. I normally have a hearty appetite at mealtime and I am always receptive to the extra treats that he sneaks to me when I get hunger pangs between breakfast and brunch, and again between dinner and my pre-bedtime snack. Any decline in my enthusiasm for food is cause for alarm. A consultation with Uncle Nigel brought forth a pronouncement that I did indeed look "a bit under the weather."

A quickly arranged appointment with the veterinarian confirmed that my discomfort was due to an infected tooth, and apparently there was no alternative but to have it removed. Further dialogue between the veterinarian and my family, Wesley and Jason on this occasion, produced words such as abscessed, surgical extraction, pre-operative radiographs, antibiotics and anaesthetic. Once the pre-op vocabulary was explained and understood by

Wesley, then came the post-op terms including potential complications, cleaning of the alveolar bone, more radiographs post-extraction, periodontal ligament, gingival flap, sutures and more antibiotics. As Wesley was digesting this information, he seemed to be calculating the corresponding monetary implication of each of these medical terms. On the ride home I overheard him say something about a second mortgage on the house.

Dr. Emerson prescribed oral antibiotics, which were to be administered to me for a day or two prior to my surgery. I won't bore you with the details of the "administering" process.

Fortunately, it was what humans call the weekend, so everyone was home and my every need was met within minutes of my uttering even the slightest mournful meow . . . which I have perfected to a science I might add. Needless to say, I was exempt from Jenna's nutritious pellets as only the softest purées were allowed to pass my lips. That luxury, however, was short-lived. On the last day before surgery I was introduced to *fasting* which in my case meant no food or water for twelve hours prior to being anaesthetized. I call it *starving*!

The weekend over and my tooth feeling much better, I was off to have my surgery. With no in-house hiding spots left, I went peacefully, wrapped in a blanket in Wesley's arms. The transportation vehicle was not required for this occasion.

Sarah was awaiting our arrival. She is the dear, sweet person who greets all animals as they arrive at the veterinarian's office. She always remembers me and calls me by name. As Wesley handed me over to her, she said that they would take good care of me and that I would be feeling better in a few days.

Dr. Emerson performed several preliminary checks . . . I wasn't exempt from the temperature-taking ordeal, but at least I didn't have an audience, as I usually do for this procedure.

My next recollection was the sensation of "wher-ezzzz . . . my body" as I only had feelings in my ears. I must have then fallen back to sleep, for when I awoke again, Sarah was beside me speaking in her soothing voice while softly stroking my head. I now had some feeling returning to my tongue but it would not stay in my mouth. Even in this semi-conscious state I had concerns that I would never again be able to consume food.

Through my still blurred vision, I saw Dr. Emerson enter the room I had heard referred to as the recovery area. After a look in my mouth, a lift of my eyelid and a few words with Sarah, I was declared "fit as a fiddle."

Time seemed to pass rather quickly. I suspect that I had slept again as it was now late afternoon I heard someone say. I was feeling somewhat better upon wakening this time, my tongue back in my mouth, eyes focusing to some degree, and I realized that I had front paws again. Sarah said that my family was in the waiting room anxiously awaiting my release.

Once home I made a valiant effort to stand, but my back half was not coordinated with my front half. For the remainder of the day and evening, family members kept a close watch over me. My food and water bowls were placed in close proximity although, as yet, I had no desire to eat.

That ordeal took place several days ago and I am now feeling well again. I have also regained my appetite with such enthusiasm that Wesley proclaimed if I didn't curb it somewhat he was going to speak to the veterinarian about having the tooth put back in.

I hope you are both well . . . or should I say I hope you are fit as fiddles.

Puurrrs,
Sugar

P.S. Your lovely gift arrived yesterday. What a pleasant surprise! Jenna said she has never seen such a pretty collar. The bright red leather and inset diamonds provide a nice contrast with my light grey fur. I especially like the way the diamonds sparkle when I turn my head from side to side. Wesley says I am true to my gender.

Sugar's Great Escape Caper

...Well, maybe not quite!

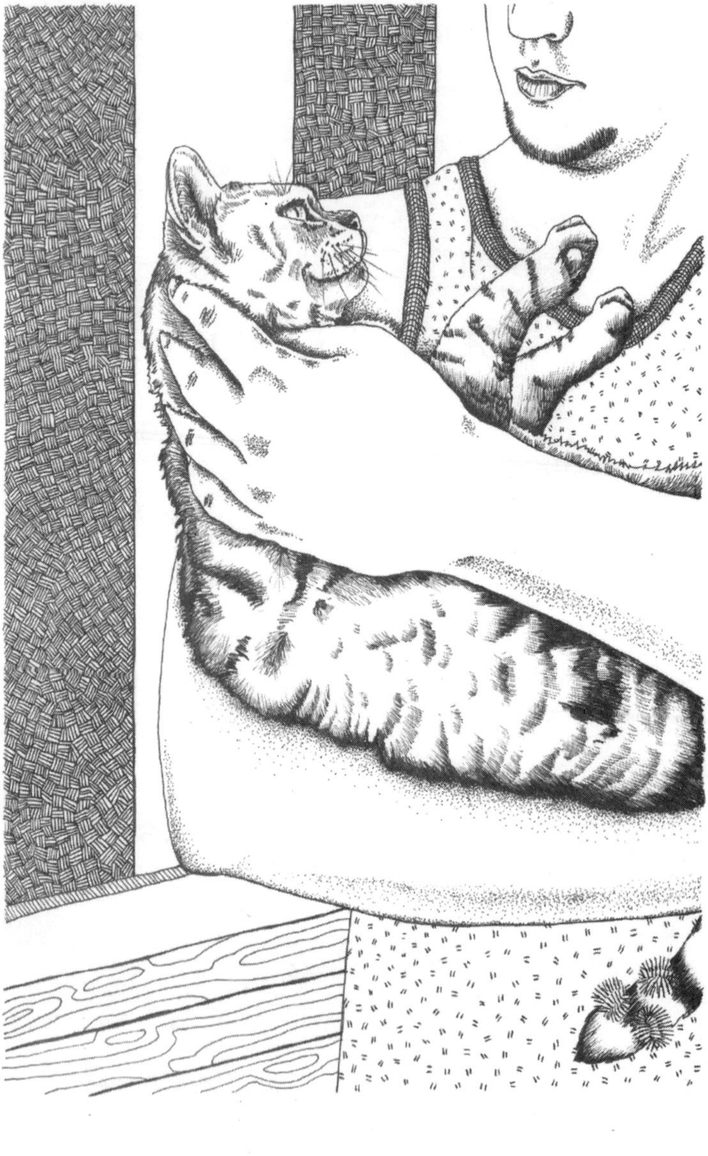

Dear Mom & Dad,

I hope that you are enjoying this welcome weather as much as I am. It is wonderful to bask in the warmth of the sun and to feel the soft grass under my paws again. The cold months of winter seem to last longer every year.

I gained some weight over the winter, but now that I am spending more time outdoors, I seem to be slimming down. Perhaps it is simply the loss of my winter fur that gives the illusion of my body being svelte again. Jason brushed me a few days ago when I was sunning myself on the deck and I heard him say that he got enough hair off of me "to make another cat." Wesley was within hearing range of that comment and I could tell by the rolling of his eyes that he was not enamoured with the idea of having another feline to contend with, even if Jason's statement was made in jest.

I think that Wesley's nerves are somewhat shattered, due primarily to two recent incidents for which I am responsible. In relating the first occurrence, I must say in my own defence that I really did not intend to frighten Wesley, but the resulting effect was nevertheless the same.

The first episode occurred several nights ago. I have my own basket with blanket for sleeping and it is generally positioned just inside the bedroom door at night. On this particular evening, it being rather cool in the house and with less fur to keep me warm, Jenna tucked me in and put another blanket over top of me. This action no doubt contributed in part to the ensuing scenario some hours later.

Rousing from a restful sleep and feeling somewhat peckish around 1:00 a.m. (the exact hour, according to Wesley as he recounts the story for the umpteenth time), I jumped onto the bed and gazed into Wesley's face from the vantage point of his upturned shoulder. My strategy was that if he "just happened" to awake, he may be inclined to get up and dole out a bit of food to tide me over until breakfast. I was totally unprepared, however, for the next turn of events in an otherwise peaceful night. Apparently, my large green eyes and the light-coloured blanket still clinging to my head and back were what Wesley saw as he stirred and peered sleepily into the semi-darkness of the room. I was suddenly propelled to the other side of the bed as he threw back the covers, simultaneously uttering the most gut wrenching *ARRRRRRAGGGGAH!* I had no idea what had just transpired. Lights came on throughout the house and I could hear running feet from all directions. To make matters worse, Jenna and Wesley had house guests.

As dawn began to appear on the horizon, I could tell that sleep was still eluding Wesley.

More recently, I was the subject of a two-and-a-half hour search by a party of five . . . again causing my family undue stress.

On the day I am describing, I had been outdoors for several hours and was becoming restless. Wesley and Jenna were engaged in conversation with our neighbours who had stopped by, and Jason and a friend were in the house working on the innards of a computer. The distractions noted, and feeling a sudden urge to explore the great beyond, I manoeuvred my way to the forest's edge. I assured myself that a quick look around would be harmless and no one would notice my absence.

Remembering Shenanigan and Kai-Bosh, the two cats I had met at the boarding kennel, I gazed around in the hopes of an encounter with them, but to no avail. I then saw Chantal, another neighbour's daughter, who was out in her backyard playing with RinGo LeRoux, their family dog. I recognized them as they have been to our house on numerous occasions. I sauntered over nonchalantly as if I frequent the outback on a regular basis.

Normally I stay away from dogs as much as possible, but I like RinGo LeRoux. He is about my size and we play and chase each other around whenever we are together. He is also one of the few canines I have encountered that doesn't have WDB (wicked dog breath). Humans will no doubt argue that there is no such thing as WDB and understandably so, since the human sense of smell is all but nonexistent compared to that of the feline species. Furthermore, humans are generally not walking around at snout level with canines.

Chantal's parents provide a foster home for abandoned animals, most of which are cats. Some need special care for medical reasons and others just need to be adopted. On warm days, they are all outdoors but confined in a large wire enclosure. I learned from one such cat named Tinkle that she was expecting her first litter of kittens and was rather frightened.

I must admit that I lost track of time with all of the activity going on. As I started back towards home, I was further distracted by some birds and a squirrel or two. Following them took me deeper into the wooded area. Suddenly, there were no homes in sight and the forest seemed to be getting denser and the air cooler. I normally have a good sense of direction but I was momentarily confused and I realized that I had been gone from home for a rather long time.

Thankfully, I heard what sounded like my name being called, but the source was quite a distance away. I hurried towards the voices but quickly realized that if I were seen arriving from beyond the boundaries of our property, a long period of house arrest would likely ensue. I couldn't let that happen — not when the warm weather had finally arrived and I could once again supplement my diet with fresh game.

As I neared the human sounds, I recognized the urgency in their voices. Each family member has a particular way of getting my attention when the need arises . . . usually when I do my disappearing act upon seeing my carry cage being extracted from the closet.

Jason was farthest into the woods yelling, "Here Shuggs!" Wesley seemed to be more to my left and his voice reflected a bit too much emphasis on the second syllable of my name as he called out, "SUG-GRRR . . ." I could see that Jenna had remained on the deck with binoculars.

It appeared that Jason's friend had departed, but the neighbours, upon hearing the distress calls, had returned and were put in charge of heavy artillery — a treat bag in each hand to be shaken every ten metres as they marched into the woods.

My fur was now standing on end as I contemplated the repercussions of my predicament.

Carefully avoiding the search party, I emerged from the underbrush on the far side of the garden shed. I crouched behind a clump of spring flowers and peered towards the back of the house hoping that the sliding door would be open a smidge and that Jenna would no longer be on the deck. No such luck!

Another possibility was that the garage at the front of the house might have been left open and perhaps the door into the basement as well. With a ray of hope propelling me, I darted along the north side of the house where no one was looking for me . . . yet!

Luckily, both doors were open, and I made a mad dash upstairs and into the farthest corner of the nearest closet.

My heart palpitations had stopped and my breathing had just become normal again when I heard someone enter the house. It happened to be Jason. My survival instincts dictated my next actions. At the appropriate moment, I stepped out of the closet, meowed softly to get his attention, yawned, stretched and sauntered over to my food bowl. How could anyone possibly think that I had been anywhere but sound asleep in the house for the past few hours?

Jason, upon seeing me, immediately went to the door and called off the search, advising everyone that I had in fact been in the house all along.

He then picked me up, cradled me in his arms, scratched my chin and murmured apologies for assuming I had left the property defying the rules, etc. etc. I was lapping it all up thinking to myself that my acting skills were worthy of a "Catamy Award" when I realized that Jason had tensed and was looking at me inquisitively. He then said, "Sugar, you *were* outside!" I blinked . . . my mind racing! How did he know? "Your paws are damp and you have burrs sticking to your tail, 'Sugar Plum.' The only place you could have gotten burrs is near the wooden bridge which is rather far from our property!" He always calls me "Sugar Plum" when he is upset with me. We stared wide-eyed at each other for a moment and I could see another of my lives flash before me. I could also hear the dismantled search party approaching the house. I am sure that Jason could see the fright on my face, for I was totally devoid of "cat caught red pawed" recovery ideas.

As we heard footsteps and voices, now on the back deck, Jason seemed to be deep in thought. He gazed down at me for a moment and then moved out of sight of the sliding door and quickly removed the telltale burrs, hiding the evidence in his pocket. Just as the sliding door opened, he whispered, "Your secret is safe this time but don't let it happen again, Miss Plum."

I will forever be indebted to Jason.

Puurrrs to you both,
Sugar

Dijon

Dear Cuda,

I was happy to hear (through the grapevine) that you and your family are once again back home in Calgary. Now that Peter has retired, your relocating days are no doubt over and you can enjoy a measure of stability in your life. Routine, nonetheless, can also become tiresome, as I have discovered.

As I indicated in my previous letter to you, I had been contented, or so I thought, with my somewhat sedentary, secure life, particularly during the months when I am confined indoors.

During our most recent long and bitterly cold winter, however, I began to experience what Jason described as "cabin fever." I would gaze day after day at the monotony of falling snow, which eventually covered every outdoor surface in sight, for what seemed to be an extraordinarily long time. My feline instincts increasingly yearned not only for the warmth of springtime, but also for the freedom to explore the wilderness without restrictions. I longed for the succulent taste of a fresh mouse, the joy of chasing butterflies and the irresistible challenge of locating well-stocked birds' nests — all of which are off limits, as decreed by my nature-loving family.

When spring finally arrived and the warm sunshine brought forth vividly coloured flowers, leaf buds, and an increase in rodent sightings, I began to spend long periods of time outdoors while post-winter cleanup was being done by Jenna and Wesley. On one such day I decided to act on my impulses, and when the opportunity arose I ventured beyond the designated boundaries of our property and into the forbidden forest. Much to my surprise I soon came upon other homes with backyards teeming with activity. Children were playing, birds were singing and my old friend RinGo LeRoux came bounding out barking a greeting. Suffice to say, it was a magical experience . . . until I realized that I had completely lost track of time and my family members were frantically searching for me. Mercifully, I survived that ordeal by a whisker . . . I won't bore you with the details!

Safely back home, my wanderlust only temporarily assuaged, I settled into a routine of sorts, periodically enjoying the reverie of my brief sojourn.

As spring dissolved into summer, I once again had an overwhelming desire for adventure. I thus began spending time as near to the woods as was permissible while remaining within the boundaries of our property. I had also determined that there was a mouse run in the vicinity of our backyard pond, and the long grass afforded a perfect camouflage for my purpose.

The temperature being warmer than usual one afternoon, I settled in to wait under a wild dogwood near the water. I soon found myself struggling to remain awake, and I was drifting towards my second nap of the day when I heard my name being called from the woods' edge. Initially I thought I must surely be dreaming, but as I lifted my head and gazed around, I detected a slight movement of the underbrush. I quickly scanned the surrounding area, my senses on full alert, fearful of encountering one of the dreaded cat-eating predators. Instead, to my astonishment, there stood a cat so handsome he took my breath away.

He was considerably larger than me with beautiful green eyes and long thick fur in a colour I had never before seen. As I gathered my thoughts I wondered, "Could *he* be meowing at *me*?" and I fervently hoped that there were no dried leaves or bits of straw clinging to the top of my head.

I acknowledged his presence by asking how he knew my name. He stepped closer and I could see that he was wearing an attractive identification collar, which indicated to me that he wasn't just a stray tomcat. As I struggled to regain my composure, he told me his name was Dijon, and he explained that he had seen me briefly one afternoon in the spring when I was visiting a neighbouring property. He had been within an enclosed area with other rescued cats and perhaps I had not noticed him, he offered. I must have been on catnip to have not noticed him, but then I had been occupied playing "chase the squirrel" with my pal RinGo.

Since then, he explained further, he had been adopted by another family nearby. Their teenage daughter Amanda had chosen him specifically because of his dark mustard and beige colouring, hence his new name, Dijon. He expressed that he must share her affection with her dog Pocket, but he is nevertheless happy to have a home of his own with a loving family.

We discovered that we had a great deal in common: he prefers mice over canned food; does not like the odour of skunks, having had an experience much like mine; and Halloween is his least favourite night of the year. Did I mention that he has a soft reassuring meow?

Dijon has been coming to visit me almost daily. I am not always outdoors of course, but he is understanding of my restrictions and he waits patiently, sometimes for hours. Seemingly, during the day he is permitted to roam freely as are many other cats that live in the area.

I am contemplating another excursion into the woods, but how I will accomplish this feat without detection by my family is yet to be determined. Any suggestions would be welcome.

Your cousin,
Sugar

P.S. I told Dijon about your bottled water experience. He would like to know if it is available in either tuna or mole flavour.

Lester

Dear Sugar,

I was delighted to receive your letter this morning, especially in view of the fact that I had not yet responded to your previous correspondence. My life has certainly been replete with changes in the past month or two, most of which have been for the better.

We have all settled in nicely since returning to our permanent home from the Far North. Retirement seems to be invigorating for Peter and Heidi and I am enjoying having them home during the day.

Heidi has redecorated the condominium with paint in uplifting colours and she and Peter have purchased some new living room furniture. The appearance of wear and tear on the previous furnishings was attributed to the frequent moves from one work location to another, when in fact I had been using the corners of sofas and chairs as my scratching posts over the years. I experienced some minor pangs of guilt until I overheard Peter complain that the now discarded pieces were only slightly more comfortable than park benches.

Not to be overlooked in the updating process, my well-travelled sleeping basket was replaced with a state-of-the-art model, complete with an overhead canopy and two fluffy new blankets, which were colour-coordinated with the new surroundings.

When we first returned to Calgary, I was fearful that my family would plan another extended holiday and I would once again have to contend with living in the same household with Lester the Pester. As time passed, however, I began to relax as I observed no signs of an impending departure.

Then one day a few weeks ago, I overheard a conversation between Heidi and Peter that virtually made my fur stand on end. Lester was coming to stay with *us*, while *his* family went on vacation. Anticipatory nausea set in immediately and I began to experience a loss of appetite and hairball issues.

On the day of his arrival, I took refuge under the king-sized bed and no amount of persuasion could get me out. I located myself mid-centre so as not to be accessible from any side. This proved frustrating for my family.

Lester arrived early afternoon with all of his belongings, for "a mere fortnight," said Heidi. Well, a fortnight is a very long time to be in his company but it is also a long time to remain under the bed. I therefore eventually relented and exited the bedroom, cautiously peering at Lester from a vantage point obscured from his view. He was gazing around the room and I surmised that he was planning his attack strategy for when our humans were out of sight and I had arrived on scene.

He appeared quite well-groomed and rather subdued. "Could this be the same Lester?" I asked myself. I decided that my approach would be neither aggressive nor friendly towards him. I would ignore him completely . . . after all it was not as if we would be sharing the same food bowl and litter box.

I finally gathered intestinal fortitude, took a deep breath, and stepped out from behind a large potted plant. My sudden appearance seemed to alarm him and he looked somewhat intimidated. Perhaps he expected the same ill treatment that he had subjected *me* to when I was a guest in *his* home. I continued past him with nary a glance in his direction. I sensed his eyes following me.

As the night progressed, my demeanor still icy cold, I sauntered over to my new basket with the intent of feigning sleep despite his presence. Thus far, I had observed no sign of aggression on his part, but Peter nevertheless relocated him to another room for the night sensing a measure of discord between us.

Day two was even more perplexing. Lester greeted me with a soft meow inquiring if I had had a restful sleep. I certainly was not about to let my guard down and fall for that ruse, so I did not reply but walked leisurely over to my food bowl giving no indication that his presence was still causing me to experience the effects of undigested hairballs.

Continuing my charade of nonchalance, I began my morning grooming routine with more enthusiasm than usual, but nevertheless keeping a close eye on him. He stood by at a non-threatening distance, and I noticed for the first time that he was actually rather handsome in a rugged sort of way. That bit of missing ear and his lopsided smile did have a certain allure. I reprimanded myself for my reckless thoughts, which were beginning to erode my better judgment.

As the day progressed, Lester tried once again to engage me in conversation. This time he offered me some of his special, certified-organic food treats, which I declined, but a hint of a somewhat friendly tone crept into my reply. Sensing a window of opportunity no doubt, he quickly continued on.

Apparently he had had an undiagnosed medical condition when he was first adopted by his present owners. He had endured a great deal of discomfort over a long period of time and only recently was pain-free with the help of proper medication and a very specialized diet. He asked my forgiveness for his despicable behaviour when I had been a guest in his home explaining that at that time he was still unwell, which had caused him to be not only irritable but downright cantankerous.

I pondered my response. Could Lester in fact be telling the truth, or was he a seasoned raconteur? I decided to reserve judgment.

For the remainder of his stay with my family he regaled me with stories of his life as a barn cat. I detected no inconsistencies in any of the narrations, and I began to understand how exposure to the cold and poor nutrition could very well cause the pain he had experienced. I learned that being a barn cat is not for the faint of heart, as he had but two of his nine lives remaining. He seemed genuinely interested in my past as well, and he again asked for my forgiveness. This time I had no hesitation and I assured him that I held no ill feelings towards him, and in fact I hoped that we would always remain friends.

The fortnight I had been dreading now seemed to have gone by much too quickly, and when Lester (I no longer call him Lester the Pester) was retrieved by his family, I was sad beyond words. I now spend my days looking longingly out the windows and desperately hoping that my family will schedule another holiday very soon.

I look forward to your next letter. Dijon sounds like quite a catch.

Your cousin,
Cuda

P.S. I don't believe the bottled water is available in anything but fruit flavours. I rather doubt that humans would be inclined to purchase mole or tuna flavoured water.

The Tobacco Shack Cats

OLD
CHUM
TOBACCO

Dear Cuda,

What wonderful developments in your life. Who would have thought that Lester and you would become such close friends. I was happy to hear that you accepted his apology and his explanation for his disagreeable behaviour. Pain can certainly cause one's good nature to erode. Several months ago I had an abscessed tooth, which was eventually extracted, but while I was enduring the pain I was not pleasant to be around.

It has been an eventful summer for me thus far. In my last letter I told you about my new friend Dijon and that we have been seeing each other almost daily. Whether I am outdoors or not, he waits patiently in our meeting spot by the pond and when I am confined to the house, I sit on the windowsill and gaze longingly into our backyard. On one such day I waited endlessly, but I didn't see him. The following day I was outdoors for several hours, but again Dijon did not appear and I began to be alarmed. Over the next few days my anxiety grew due to his continued absence, and my appetite diminished. I think the mice sensed my lack of interest as they scurried around taunting me in the long grass.

My disinterest in food was also noted by Jenna and she seemed to be observing me more closely, which was a detriment, since I was determined to enter the woods in the hope of finding the location of Dijon's new home.

An opportunity presented itself mid-morning on the fifth day. I was again sitting near the pond when I heard the faint sound of the telephone ringing and I saw Jenna rushing towards the house. I am still rather agile so I surmised that I could enter the woods, hopefully find Dijon's home, and return to the pond without my absence being detected.

I was barely halfway through the woods, however, when I heard cat chatter coming from a dilapidated tobacco storage facility that I had not noticed on my previous escapade. My heart pounding, I raced towards the building in the hope that Dijon was among the cats inside. As I peered through an opening in the back wall, I was delighted to see Kai-Bosh and Shenanigan, the cats I had met during my brief stay at the Bulrush Kennel. I recognized another cat named Tinkle, although she was much slimmer having had her kittens since I last saw her. There were also several other cats I had not seen before, but much to my disappointment Dijon was not there. I nevertheless made my presence known in the hope that one of them would know where I might find him.

Kai-Bosh and Shenanigan made a huge fuss over me and introductions were made around the rafters. Kai-Bosh made a slight faux "paw" when he introduced me as "Sweet" instead of "Sugar" but a light kick to his ribs by Shenanigan alerted him to his mistake. He made a valiant attempt at a recovery by saying that he remembered me as a "sweet" cat so hence the mistake. What a charmer!

Tinkle said she remembered our brief meeting in the spring. She too had been adopted by a local family.

I learned that the cats had formed a club aptly named The Tobacco Shack Cats and I was provided a bit of background about each of the members. Merlot was the senior feline and seemed to enjoy the status. Ping Pong, a multi-coloured female, was rather shy and said very little. The Himalayan Persian beauty named Mirage stayed well away from the other cats fearing a possible encounter with a flea. Another member named Ebony was absent. Taco, I learned, had been a stray for most of his life and enjoyed entertaining club members with harrowing tales of his adventures. He was proud of his nickname "Scrapper."

I once again lost track of time. In panic mode I raced from the building assuring them that I would return shortly. Although obscured from view due to the dense foliage, the tobacco shack is really quite near my home.

I have become quite adept at my *flat cat* stance when I don't want my presence detected, hence was my approach as I neared our pond. Jenna was having lunch in the gazebo and seemingly was not aware of my absence. I sauntered over in her direction swatting at a non-existent object in the air, ensuring that she would notice me. I then settled down on the far side of a shrub so that I could once again slip away when she returned to the garden. I had a brief pang of guilt at my devious behaviour but I could not miss an opportunity to find Dijon.

My guilt was compounded when Jenna, upon finishing her lunch, brought me a bowl of fresh water, stroked my head and told me that I was a very good cat.

A short while later I manoeuvred my way towards the outer edge of the property, through the long grass, and into the woods. I was welcomed again by my new friends and I immediately asked if anyone knew Dijon. They all said they did know him but had not seen him for several days. I was distraught. Had his family moved away, or perhaps he was ill?

I then asked if anyone knew where Dijon's new family lived and I was promptly escorted to his backyard, but we could see no indication that anyone was there. I returned home with a heavy heart and Jenna seemed to sense that something was wrong. I rubbed against her legs and she picked me up and hugged me. "Ah Shuggums," she said, using her favourite endearment for me.

Once indoors and nearing exhaustion at this point, I succumbed to sleep soon after settling into my basket. I was awakened a few hours later when Jason arrived home. He made his way to the aft deck via the kitchen securing a handful of freshly made cookies along the way. Then I heard him call to Jenna, "Mom, do you know who owns the large orange cat sitting in our yard?" *Yeeeeesssss!* Now fully awake, I raced through the open door and down the steps — Jason in hot pursuit, assuming that a full-fledged, fur-flying cat fight would ensue. Dijon, throwing caution to the wind, came bounding towards me, substantiating Jason's fears momentarily. Just as Jason was about to scoop me up, however, Dijon and I went skipping across the lawn showing no sign of aggression towards each other. By now Jenna too was outdoors and she and Jason exchanged looks of disbelief.

When we reached the pond, Dijon explained that his family had gone on a short vacation and that they had taken him to the nearby boarding kennel. He had had no prior knowledge of their departure and therefore could not inform me.

The following day when we met, Dijon said that the neighbourhood cats had invited us to a *pawt-luck* dinner at the tobacco shack to celebrate his return, and also to meet Shadow, the Himalayan kitten who was the new addition to Mirage's family. With little time to prepare, I contributed dessert in the form of two catnip-filled mice that I had received as gifts.

Although I could not stay long at the event, I nevertheless had a wonderful time. Little Shadow was the centre of attention despite his shyness and reluctance to leave Mirage's side. My maternal instincts still intact, I silently wished that my family would adopt a kitten for me as well.

Before we left, Dijon and I were invited to join The Tobacco Shack Cats along with another cat whose family recently moved to our neighbourhood. Her name is Atlantis but she is better known by her nom de plume "Tabby." We were all delighted to learn that we have a celebrity among us, as she is the feline columnist who writes the "Dear Tabby" advice column for cats. We have all been asked to submit our most daunting dilemmas so that she can kick-start her writing at her new place of employment, *The Paw Print Observer*.

In closing, I have some potentially good news for you. I have heard that Peter and Heidi will be visiting friends and family in our area this summer. I will keep my paws crossed that you will be seeing Lester again.

Puurrrs,
Sugar

Dear Tabby

PAW PRINT
OBSERVER
Dear Tabby,

Dear Tabby,

I am a founding member of a feline club called The Tobacco Shack Cats (TTSC). We have all been adopted by loving families and have good homes. Each of us, however, has made an observation about our humans, and that is their disregard for basic hygiene etiquette. We are appalled that, unlike felines, humans never lick their hands to clean their faces or behind their ears after consuming food. This is elementary training taught to us as kittens. Should we be concerned that bacteria could be transferred to us when they pick us up or pat our heads?
Merlot, SeCATary, TTSC

Dear Merlot,

Humans are not as self-sufficient as we felines and therefore must rely on other means for personal grooming. Most will take precautions when eating so as not to leave food deposits on their faces and they will generally use soap and water to clean their hands both before and after consuming food. Your concerns are unfounded. There is no need to lose a catnap over it.

Dear Tabby,

I have been an outdoor cat all of my life, but now that I'm getting on in years I have decided to accept the kindness of a human family that has offered me food and shelter. Being confined to the indoors overnight, however, requires me to use something called a litter box for my personal needs. Tabby, this thing is frightening! Out of desperation one night, I stepped into it and made a small deposit. I quickly covered it as I would if I were outdoors but the more I tried to mask it the larger it became. What is it? I lie awake every night in fear of having to step into the box again.
Taco (Scrapper)

Dear Scrapper,

Humans have invented a product called litter, which is specifically for, as you indicated, "feline needs" when outdoor facilities are not accessible. It is perfectly safe to use. The product is available in many different forms. Some are scented, others unscented; clumping and non-clumping are other options and most are dust free. The one you have encountered is likely the clumping variety, which totally adheres to any moisture with which it makes contact, thus increasing the size of the original deposit, sometimes quite substantially. Sleep tight! Don't worry about the box.

Dear Tabby,

By my own admission, I have been a pampered cat all of my life. I was adopted as a kitten and have been with the same family for several years. I am Himalayan Persian and I have always been admired for my beauty. Middle age is setting in, however, and I have recently been considering some cosmetic procedures to maintain my youthful appearance. A friend had a fur lift and a tail bob with some degree

of success, but I have lived a rather sedentary life and I feel that a more drastic procedure may be required. Is there such a thing as liposuction for cats?
Mirage

Dear Mirage,

I am opposed to any type of cosmetic surgery for felines. Daily exercise would be a better option. Chase a ball, roll on your back from side to side, or jump in the air as if attempting to catch a fly. You could even try your paw at catching a real mouse, but if you are successful don't consume it as it will add to your daily intake of calories.

Dear Tabby,

My previous human family moved to another country recently, and due to my advanced age, quarantine restrictions, and other "red tape" as they called it, they chose to leave me behind with the family who purchased their house. I am delighted with this arrangement as my new family includes two young children who spend time with me, and I am allowed to sleep on their beds. The problem is …

I don't understand a word they say. The children call me "Minou Noir," although my name is Ebony, and they seem to think that I am deaf because I don't respond when they talk to me. I am very confused, what could be the problem?
Ebony

Dear Ebony,

First, I must say that your previous owners were thoughtful in not subjecting you to a long journey and all of the emotional upheaval that is involved in relocating to another country.

I believe the situation that exists in your current home is that your new family speaks a different language, probably French. Unlike the feline species, which has universally recognized methods of conveying information, humans communicate by speaking, and there are several thousand different languages spoken around the world. Most humans speak and understand only one, although there are exceptions. Be patient, you will eventually learn to interpret the new-sounding words.

Dear Tabby,

I am writing this on behalf of my friend Tinkle who has not had much practice using a computer, plus she has her paws full as a new mother with three small kittens. She would like some advice with regard to a rather delicate matter within her home.

Tinkle was adopted just prior to the birth of her kittens. Out of concern for her well-being her new family placed her "birthing basket" and personal-need items in their bedroom. Their rationale being that should she encounter a problem delivering her kittens during the night they would be available to help. She is grateful for their kindness but herein lies the problem: her humans snore so loudly she is unable to sleep.

The situation is now compounded. The kittens are a few weeks old but the basket is still in their bedroom and they too are unable to sleep and they meow endlessly. She has tried to relocate them to another room but her humans, not realizing the problem, return them to the basket and close the bedroom door. Is there any solution?

I am ever so grateful that no one in my human family inherited the snore gene.

Sugar

Dear Sugar,

This is a common problem I am asked about frequently. There does not appear to be any one solution that is effective in all cases. Loud, persistent meowing is usually sufficiently disruptive to rouse the sleeping person(s) and, therefore, quell the "offending noise"— for a while! It has been pointed out, however, that the offending noise is sometimes so substantial that the meow is ineffective. Some readers have achieved a measure of success by scratching or nipping an exposed arm or leg of the sleeping individual(s). This approach, however, requires great skill and agility!

Spice

Dear Mom & Dad,

This has been the most eventful and wonderful summer of my life. I have so many exciting things to tell you, but first I would like to thank you for the two catnip-filled mice you sent me. They are so realistic in appearance that Wesley was startled when one mysteriously found its way into one of his slippers! It is fortunate for me that Wesley has a good sense of humour, otherwise he may have vetoed the surprise that the family had planned for me.

Several days ago my feline intuition began sensing something happening that I was not to know about. Phone conversations were hushed or stopped abruptly when I entered the room. Family members were exchanging looks with each other and a lot of smiling was going on when they looked my way.

Then one evening when Wesley and Jenna left for their usual after-dinner walk, they took my carry cage with them. To say that I was mystified would be an understatement. I gazed up at Jason as they were leaving but his "poker face" revealed nothing, although in retrospect, I think I did detect a hint of mischief in his eyes.

My curiosity burdened my attempt to sleep as I tried desperately to think of a situation that would necessitate them taking my carry cage. I finally appeased my mind with two possible scenarios. One being that the neighbourhood was fundraising by having a carry cage wash rather than the customary car wash, or secondly, and the less desirable of the two probabilities, was that they were exchanging it for a larger one, necessitated by my recent girth expansion due to middle-age spread.

Jason seemed restless awaiting their return but the wait was soon over. Wesley arrived at the door with the still empty cage in hand followed by Jenna who was carrying what appeared to be a small grey kitten. I was truly overjoyed by this unexpected surprise.

Not knowing what my reaction would be, my family was cautious when introducing me to the new arrival. All in attendance quickly realized, however, that they had miscalculated. It was I who needed protection! As I approached the little tabby to welcome him, I was rewarded with a stinging sensation on the upper part of my nose. I quickly backed away but the little needle-like claws remained affixed to my nostrils. Wesley came to my rescue and disengaged the miniature paw from my face.

Spice, as he has been named, is a bundle of energy and no moving object goes unnoticed . . . especially my tail. Although he has his own sleeping basket, he insists on sharing mine, which is quite alright except for the fact that our sleeping schedules are opposite, and I am beginning to exhibit signs of sleep deprivation.

Much to my delight, I learned that Spice is one of Tinkle's kittens. As I mentioned in an earlier letter, Tinkle and I met briefly in the spring when she was pregnant. We now see each other quite frequently.

Another source of joy in my life is the friendship that has developed with a very charming, handsome cat named Dijon whom I met this summer. He visits me daily and through him I have met other cats in the neighbourhood. I am now a member of their club called The Tobacco Shack Cats. I cannot participate in many club functions due to my territorial restrictions but I do manage to slip away occasionally as the clubhouse is not far from our property boundary.

I have also become reacquainted with Kai-Bosh and Shenanigan whom, as you will recall, I met when I was at the Bulrush Boarding Kennel last year. They have not lost their ability to keep the feline population entertained and humans bewildered.

Their most recent caper, although well-intentioned, had near disastrous results for several of the local feline population — myself included.

The sequence of events began a short while ago when Mirage, who is a club member, began fretting about her weight gain. Still possessing the beauty of her Himalayan heritage, her concerns seemed unfounded but she was determined to undergo a rather drastic body-altering procedure. Enter Kai-Bosh and Shenanigan with a plan by which Mirage could regain her once youthful figure without intrusive surgery.

Bosh and Nan, as they are known among club

members, live in close proximity to the clubhouse. Their human caregiver named Oliver is something of a self-proclaimed Mr. Fix-it of the neighbourhood, when not working at his long-time employment at the local assembly plant. His property, therefore, includes an oversized workshop which is fully equipped with tools of the trade. Within the shop is a very large circular table that has been modified to Oliver's specifications. With the press of a lever, the table surface moves laterally completing one rotation every fifty-six seconds. Seemingly, after years of working on an assembly line, Oliver is unable to work on a stationary surface.

With Oliver not yet home from work, all club members were invited to the workshop one afternoon to witness Bosh and Nan's plan put into action. With all of us displaying varying degrees of agility, we positioned ourselves on shelves, tool boxes and stacks of tires, or anything else that would afford an advantageous view of the mysterious table. Mirage was initially reluctant to enter the workshop fearing an encounter with a spot of grease, but she eventually relented, and when invited to be the first to try out the table, she did so with a flick of her tail and toss of her head. As the lever was pressed and the surface began to move she walked against the rotation. The workshop erupted with the sound of meows and yowls as Mirage tested the "treadmill." Eventually, we all leapt onto the table enjoying the activity, which became competitive as we raced to see who would be first to complete the circle. Kai-Bosh and Shenanigan stood back, their signature grins reflecting another successful accomplishment.

All was well until the sound of a truck door slamming sent all participants fleeing for cover. When Oliver entered the workshop there was not a feline in sight and the only sound was the whirr of the table surface as it continued to rotate. Peering out from behind a lawn mower, I observed Oliver, hat in hand, scratching his head as he mumbled something about having been sure that he had turned off the mechanism.

The table now silenced, Oliver exited the shop, closing the door and to our horror, locking it as well. As we heard the sound of the truck driving away, we all emerged from our various hiding places with looks of disbelief on our faces.

Collective thoughts were unspoken. "What if Oliver did not return for several days, or a week…or longer?" Mirage became hysterical. She wailed that she could not stand another minute in this dustbin . . . her fur would lose it lustre forever! My fear was that I would starve to death. Dijon tried unsuccessfully to calm everyone. Taco, being accustomed to the freedom of the outdoors, was claustrophobic, and poor Tinkle fretted that she would never again see her kittens. Merlot and Ping Pong, the more mature felines of the group, proceeded to inspect the locking mechanism on the door.

Through all of this Kai-Bosh and Shenanigan were huddled together obviously deep in thought. This was an unexpected turn of events.

Dijon took it upon himself to explore the interior of the building in the hope of finding an alternate exit. Unfortunately, the only other door was a large roll-up variety that could accommodate a vehicle. It too was securely closed. A single window in the shop was located beside the door and it was obvious that it too would not assure our freedom.

By now I was approaching a state of panic. It seemed like hours had elapsed since I had left home. The fear of starving to death was being overshadowed by the fear of permanent house arrest should my transgression be discovered, which it would be I had no doubt.

Merlot, having some authority as seCATary for the club, took charge. She assigned Ping Pong to console Mirage . . . preferably away from the group so that "the rest of us can think straight." She then asked each of us to close our eyes for a period of time and visualize a possible solution to our dilemma.

When the allotted time was up, Taco was first to offer a suggestion. "Perhaps we could dig a hole under the foundation," he said. Merlot thanked him for the idea but pointed out that the entire surface of the floor was made of cement. Tinkle, through her sobs, thought we should all meow simultaneously in the hope that someone might hear us and come to our rescue. Everyone nodded in agreement that the idea did indeed have some merit, but there could be consequences if our respective families were informed of our reckless behaviour.

Dijon asked if he could have another look around the shop in the hope of something prompting an idea. When all eyes turned in my direction, I felt a hairball stir within my stomach and the discomfort prevented me from uttering a sound. Sensing my embarrassment, Kai-Bosh cleared his throat and said that he and Shenanigan had a plan . . . all eyes rolled in unison! Merlot reminded everyone that we had few options at this point and we should be receptive to any and all suggestions.

Kai-Bosh continued, outlining their plan. Each cat would be assigned to a piece of equipment in the shop. Every attempt should be made to activate the start mechanisms if it could be done so by the flip of a toggle switch, push of a button or press of a lever. We would obviously be exempt from devices with pull cords, thus eliminating the two chain saws and the lawn mower. If we were successful, the resulting noise would most certainly bring Oliver back to the shop. The final phase of the plan would be to ensure our presence was not detected. We therefore must remain hidden until Oliver was engaged in turning off the machinery, at which time we could cautiously vacate the premises with reputations intact.

Merlot pointed out that one of us would be required to sit at the window to watch for Oliver. Thus far, I had not been at all helpful and wanting to impress my fellow club members, I quickly volunteered. I soon had second thoughts, however, when I realized that reaching the sill would be a challenge . . . even for a cat.

Additional furballs rumbled in my stomach as I searched the surrounding area for something from which I could propel myself in order to gain access to the narrow ledge of the window. The only thing in sight was a thick rope dangling overhead between the large exit door and the window. It seemed to have no purpose, but I thought perhaps it would suffice for my immediate need . . . if it could sustain my excess avoirdupois. I also had to leap high enough to grasp the end, which was hanging a substantial distance off the floor.

My audience watched in stunned silence as I became airborne, paws extended and heart thumping. My front claws had barely lodged into the knot at the end of the rope when a loud rumble erupted from nearby. To everyone's amazement, the large door began to move slowly upwards and I began to move downwards. The spectators scattered in all directions. Panic set in as I tried desperately to retract my claws from the rope with one thought racing through my mind, "Surely Oliver had returned and I will no doubt be tarred and feathered!"

As I gained my freedom from the rope and my feet made contact with the cement floor, the shop fell silent once again, the large door now fully open.

Oliver, thankfully, was nowhere in sight. Small furry heads began to peer out from behind various objects. I stood motionless in front of the wide open door paralyzed with fear; the stance mistakenly interpreted as bravery by my fellow felines — a perception I have yet to dispel.

Fur flying would be how I would describe the scene as we vacated the workshop. How the rope related to the opening of the door will forever remain a mystery.

Back home, I cautiously approached the boundary of our property. Surely Jenna, Wesley and Jason would be frantically searching for me once again. Had I not been gone for hours? Apparently not. As I gazed around, I realized that the sun had moved very little since my departure and my favourite shady spots remained intact. Wesley had not yet finished mowing the backyard lawn and Jenna was still working on cleaning the two bird baths. Obviously my hair-raising experience had distorted my perception of the passage of time.

Spice, despite his young age, was aware that I had been gone for a short while and only he recognized that I had endured a traumatic episode.

I feel so fortunate to have not one, but two very loving human families and now with the addition of another feline to share my home, I feel my life is complete.

Please visit again soon. Spice is looking forward to meeting you.

Love & Puurrrs,
Sugar & Spice

Acknowledgements

First and foremost *Letters from Sugar* would never have been written were it not for family and friends who persuaded me to publish my "Sugar Letters." Thank you for spawning the idea which resulted in my taking up the challenge.

I am grateful to Shelley Richardson (EDDY Press) for her invaluable guidance as I embarked on my new venture into the publishing world. Sarah Wilkes, thank you for confirming the medical terminology and procedures used in describing a feline tooth extraction and for the TLC you extend to all the animals in your care.

It was my good fortune to find the very talented and creative artist/illustrator, Lesley Bergen whose illustrations have brought the pages of the book to life.

The collective efforts of all who have contributed in some way to the finished product came together through Marijke Friesen's expertise with design.

Marnie Ferguson, my publisher, editor and all around "go to person," is an absolute treasure with infinite patience.

Last, but certainly not least, my love and gratitude to my immediate family members for their support, encouragement and good humour during those times when I was immobilized by near terminal "writer's block."

JOYCE ERNYES is the author of *Letters from Sugar*, her first published work of fiction. She was born in a small town in Quebec where she spent her early childhood. Being an only child, her companions were very often the beloved family cat and dog. Her fondness for animals continued in her adult life and she worked with various organizations for the prevention of cruelty to animals. During her many years as a flight attendant she travelled extensively, often to remote areas of Africa where she enjoyed photographing and observing animals in their natural habitat. Her wings clipped in semi–retirement, she now lives with her family in New Lowell, Ontario.

Lesley Bergen realized her love of art at an early age. Her illustrations and artwork focus primarily on drawing and painting domestic interiors. Lesley works in acrylics, pen and ink as well as digital art. She lives with her family in Calgary, Alberta. To learn more about Lesley and her art, visit her website, lesleypaints.ca.